NORMAN BYRD

The DeFi Handbook

Step-by-Step Strategies for Earning, Borrowing, and Trading in the Decentralized Economy

First published by Norman Byrd 2025

First edition

This book was professionally typeset on Reedsy.
Find out more at reedsy.com

Contents

Introduction

Welcome to the Decentralized Future

Imagine a world where you can earn interest on your savings without relying on a bank, borrow money without filling out endless paperwork, or invest in cutting-edge financial products without needing permission from anyone. A world where financial systems are open, transparent, and accessible to everyone—no matter where they live or how much money they have. This is not a distant utopia; it's the reality being built today through *Decentralized*

Finance, or *DeFi*.

DeFi is revolutionizing the way we think about money, banking, and investing. By leveraging blockchain technology, DeFi eliminates the need for intermediaries like banks and brokers, putting the power of finance directly into your hands. Whether you're looking to earn passive income, borrow funds, or explore innovative investment opportunities, DeFi offers a world of possibilities. But with great power comes great responsibility—and understanding how to navigate this new frontier is key to unlocking its potential.

This book, *"DeFi Unlocked: How to Earn, Borrow, and Invest in the Decentralized Future,"* is your guide to this exciting and rapidly evolving space. Whether you're a complete beginner curious about crypto or an experienced investor looking to dive deeper into DeFi, this book will equip you with the knowledge and tools you need to succeed. We'll start with the basics, breaking down complex concepts like blockchain and smart contracts into simple, easy-to-understand terms. From there, we'll explore the many ways you can participate in DeFi—from earning interest on your crypto to borrowing funds and trading on decentralized exchanges.

But *DeFi isn't without its risks*. The space is still young, and with innovation comes uncertainty. That's why we'll also cover the potential pitfalls of DeFi, from smart contract vulnerabilities to regulatory challenges, and provide practical tips to help you stay safe while navigating this new landscape.

By the end of this book, you'll not only understand how DeFi works but also feel confident exploring it on your own. You'll discover how to:

- Earn passive income through yield farming, staking, and liquidity mining.
- Borrow and lend crypto securely on decentralized platforms.
- Trade assets on decentralized exchanges (DEXs) without intermediaries.
- Spot opportunities and avoid common risks in the DeFi ecosystem.

The decentralized future is here, and it's full of opportunities for those willing to learn and adapt. Whether you're looking to grow your wealth, gain financial independence, or simply be part of a groundbreaking movement,

DeFi has something to offer. But like any powerful tool, it requires knowledge and caution to use effectively. That's where this book comes in.

So, are you ready to take control of your financial future? To explore a world where the rules of finance are being rewritten? To unlock the potential of DeFi and join the ranks of those shaping the future of money? If so, turn the page—and let's begin this journey together.

Welcome to the decentralized future. It's yours to explore!

Chapter 1: Understanding the Basics of Blockchain and Cryptocurrency

Before we dive into the exciting world of Decentralized Finance (DeFi), it's essential to understand the foundation upon which it's built: *blockchain technology* and *cryptocurrency*. Think of blockchain as the engine that powers DeFi, and cryptocurrency as the fuel that makes it run. Don't worry if these terms sound intimidating—by the end of this chapter, you'll have a clear understanding of how they work and why they're so revolutionary.

What is Blockchain? The Digital Ledger Revolution

Imagine a notebook that records every transaction ever made, but instead of being stored in one place, this notebook is copied and shared across thousands of computers worldwide. That's essentially what a blockchain is—a decentralized, digital ledger that records transactions in a secure, transparent, and tamper-proof way.

Here's how it works:

1. *Blocks:* Transactions are grouped into "blocks." For example, if Alice sends Bob 1 Bitcoin, that transaction is added to a block.
2. *Chain:* Each block is linked to the one before it, creating a "chain" of blocks—hence the name *blockchain*.
3. *Decentralization:* Instead of being controlled by a single entity (like a

bank), the blockchain is maintained by a network of computers (called nodes) that work together to validate and record transactions.

Why is this revolutionary? Because it eliminates the need for intermediaries. You don't need a bank to send money or a lawyer to verify a contract. The blockchain does it all, securely and transparently.

Key Concepts: Decentralization, Smart Contracts, and Consensus

To truly grasp blockchain, let's break down three key concepts: *decentralization, smart contracts,* and *consensus mechanisms*. These are the pillars that make blockchain technology so revolutionary, and understanding them is crucial to unlocking the potential of DeFi.

1. Decentralization: Power to the People

In traditional systems, power is concentrated in the hands of a few. Banks, governments, and corporations act as intermediaries, controlling access to financial services, data, and resources. While these systems have worked for centuries, they come with significant drawbacks: high fees, slow transactions, lack of transparency, and vulnerability to censorship or corruption.

Blockchain flips this model on its head by introducing decentralization. Instead of relying on a single authority, blockchain distributes control across a network of computers (called nodes). Each node has a copy of the entire blockchain, and they work together to validate and record transactions. This creates a system that is:

- *Transparent:* Anyone can view the blockchain and verify transactions.
- *Secure:* Because the data is distributed, it's nearly impossible to hack or alter.

- *Resistant to Censorship:* No single entity can control or shut down the network.

Example: Imagine you want to send money to a friend in another country. With a traditional bank, you'd have to pay high fees, wait days for the transaction to clear, and trust the bank to handle it correctly. With blockchain, you can send cryptocurrency directly to your friend in minutes, with minimal fees, and without needing to trust a middleman.

2. Smart Contracts: The Building Blocks of DeFi

Smart contracts are one of the most exciting innovations enabled by blockchain technology. Think of them as self-executing agreements written in code. Once certain conditions are met, the contract automatically executes the agreed-upon actions—no intermediaries, no delays, and no room for human error. How they work:

- A smart contract is programmed with specific rules (e.g., "If X happens, then do Y").
- Once deployed on the blockchain, it cannot be altered.
- When the conditions are met, the contract executes automatically.

Example 1: Renting an Apartment

Let's say you want to rent an apartment. Traditionally, you'd need to sign a lease, pay a deposit, and trust the landlord to return your deposit when you move out. With a smart contract, you could program the following:

- If the tenant pays the deposit, transfer the digital keys to the apartment.
- If the tenant moves out and leaves the apartment in good condition, automatically return the deposit.

This eliminates the need for a middleman (like a rental agency) and ensures both parties are treated fairly.

Example 2: Crowdfunding

Imagine you're launching a Kickstarter campaign. Traditionally, you'd rely on the platform to collect funds and release them to you once your goal is met. With a smart contract, you could program the following:

- If the funding goal is reached by a certain date, release the funds to the project creator.
- If the goal isn't met, automatically refund the backers.

This creates a trustless system where backers don't have to worry about their money being misused.

3. Consensus Mechanisms: How Blockchain Stays in Sync

One of the biggest challenges in a decentralized system is ensuring that everyone agrees on the state of the ledger. How do all those nodes in the network decide which transactions are valid and which aren't? This is where consensus mechanisms come in. They are the rules that govern how nodes reach agreement, ensuring the integrity and security of the blockchain.

Proof of Work (PoW):

Used by Bitcoin, PoW is the original consensus mechanism. Here's how it works:

- Nodes (called miners) compete to solve complex mathematical puzzles.
- The first miner to solve the puzzle gets to add a new block of transactions to the blockchain and is rewarded with cryptocurrency.
- This process is energy-intensive but highly secure, as altering a block would require redoing all the work that came after it.

Example: Think of PoW like a race where miners are solving Sudoku puzzles. The first one to finish gets a prize, and everyone else checks their work to make sure it's correct.

Proof of Stake (PoS):

PoS is a more energy-efficient alternative to PoW. Here's how it works:

- Validators are chosen to create new blocks based on the amount of cryptocurrency they "stake" (lock up) as collateral.
- The more cryptocurrency a validator stakes, the higher their chances of being selected.
- If a validator acts dishonestly, they risk losing their staked funds.

Example: Imagine a lottery where your chances of winning depend on how many tickets you buy. In PoS, the more cryptocurrency you stake, the more "tickets" you have.

Other Consensus Mechanisms:

- *Delegated Proof of Stake (DPoS):* Token holders vote for delegates who validate transactions on their behalf.
- *Proof of Authority (PoA):* A small number of trusted nodes are given the authority to validate transactions.
- *Proof of History (PoH):* Used by Solana, this mechanism timestamps transactions to improve efficiency.

Why These Concepts Matter

Decentralization, smart contracts, and consensus mechanisms are the backbone of blockchain technology—and by extension, DeFi. Together, they enable a financial system that is:

- *Open:* Anyone with an internet connection can participate.

- *Transparent:* All transactions are recorded on a public ledger.
- *Efficient:* Smart contracts automate processes, reducing the need for intermediaries.
- *Secure:* Consensus mechanisms ensure the integrity of the network.

What is Cryptocurrency? Digital Money for the Internet Age

Cryptocurrency is the native currency of blockchain networks. It's digital money that exists purely in the digital world, secured by cryptography (hence the name *crypto*). Unlike traditional currencies, which are issued and regulated by governments, cryptocurrencies operate on decentralized networks, making them immune to government interference or manipulation. The first and most famous cryptocurrency is *Bitcoin,* created in 2009 by an anonymous person (or group) known as Satoshi Nakamoto. But Bitcoin is just the beginning—there are now thousands of cryptocurrencies, each with its own unique features and use cases.

Let's dive deeper into what makes cryptocurrency so revolutionary and why it's often referred to as "digital money for the internet age."

Decentralized: Money Without Middlemen

One of the most defining features of cryptocurrency is its decentralization. Traditional currencies, like the US dollar or the Euro, are controlled by central banks and governments. These institutions have the power to print more money, set interest rates, and impose regulations. While this centralized control can provide stability, it also comes with drawbacks: inflation, fees, and limited access for those without bank accounts.

Cryptocurrencies, on the other hand, are decentralized. They operate on blockchain networks that are maintained by a distributed network of computers (nodes) around the world. No single entity—whether a government, bank, or corporation—has control over the network. This decentralization brings several key benefits:

- *No Intermediaries:* You can send cryptocurrency directly to anyone, anywhere, without needing a bank or payment processor.
- *Censorship Resistance:* Governments or institutions can't freeze or seize your funds (as long as you control your private keys).
- *Financial Inclusion:* Cryptocurrencies provide access to financial services for the unbanked and underbanked populations worldwide.

In countries with unstable currencies or strict capital controls, like Venezuela or Argentina, people have turned to Bitcoin as a way to preserve their wealth and bypass government restrictions. They can store their savings in Bitcoin and transfer funds internationally without relying on banks.

Limited Supply: A Hedge Against Inflation

Another key feature of many cryptocurrencies is their limited supply. Traditional fiat currencies, like the US dollar, can be printed in unlimited quantities by central banks. While this can stimulate economic growth, it also leads to inflation, eroding the purchasing power of money over time.

Cryptocurrencies like Bitcoin are designed to be deflationary. Bitcoin has a fixed supply of 21 million coins, meaning no more than 21 million Bitcoins will ever exist. This scarcity is built into the protocol and enforced by the blockchain. As a result, Bitcoin is often compared to "digital gold"—a store of value that can protect against inflation.

Imagine you had $100 in 2000. Due to inflation, that $100 would only be worth about $50 in today's dollars. But if you had invested that $100 in Bitcoin in 2010 (when it was worth less than a dollar), it would be worth millions today. While this is an extreme example, it illustrates the potential of cryptocurrencies as a hedge against inflation.

Global and Borderless: Money Without Borders

Cryptocurrencies are global and borderless, meaning they can be sent and received anywhere in the world, instantly and with minimal fees. This is a game-changer for international transactions, which are often slow, expensive, and subject to exchange rate fluctuations when using traditional banking systems. Here's why this matters:

- *Speed:* Cryptocurrency transactions can be completed in minutes, regardless of where the sender and receiver are located.
- *Low Fees:* Sending cryptocurrency typically costs a fraction of what banks or services like Western Union charge.
- *No Exchange Rates:* Cryptocurrencies like Bitcoin are the same everywhere, so you don't have to worry about converting currencies.

Imagine you're a freelancer in India working for a client in the United States. Traditionally, you'd have to wait days for a bank transfer, pay high fees, and lose money to currency conversion. With cryptocurrency, you can receive payment in Bitcoin or another crypto instantly, with minimal fees, and convert it to your local currency if needed.

Beyond Bitcoin: A World of Cryptocurrencies

While Bitcoin is the most well-known cryptocurrency, it's just the tip of the iceberg. There are now thousands of cryptocurrencies, each with its own unique features and use cases. Here are a few examples:

1. *Ethereum (ETH):* Often referred to as the "world computer," Ethereum is a blockchain platform that enables smart contracts and decentralized applications (dApps). Its native currency, Ether, is used to power transactions and computations on the network.

2. *Ripple (XRP):* Designed for fast and low-cost international payments, Ripple is used by banks and financial institutions to facilitate cross-border transactions.
3. *Litecoin (LTC):* Created as the "silver to Bitcoin's gold," Litecoin offers faster transaction times and lower fees, making it ideal for everyday purchases.
4. *Stablecoins (e.g., USDT, USDC):* These cryptocurrencies are pegged to stable assets like the US dollar, providing the benefits of crypto (speed, low fees) without the volatility.
5. *Utility Tokens:* Many cryptocurrencies are designed for specific purposes, such as accessing services on a platform (e.g., Filecoin for decentralized storage) or participating in governance (e.g., MakerDAO's MKR token).

Cryptocurrency is more than just a new form of money—it's a paradigm shift in how we think about value, trust, and financial systems. By combining decentralization, limited supply, and global accessibility, cryptocurrencies offer a powerful alternative to traditional finance. Whether you're looking to protect your wealth from inflation, send money across borders, or participate in the growing world of DeFi, cryptocurrency provides the tools to do so.

As we move further into the digital age, cryptocurrencies are poised to play an increasingly important role in our lives. In the next chapter, we'll explore how these digital currencies come together with blockchain technology to create the world of Decentralized Finance (DeFi). So, let's keep going—the future of money is just getting started!

How Blockchain Enables DeFi

Now that you understand blockchain and cryptocurrency, let's connect the dots to *DeFi (Decentralized Finance).* DeFi is essentially a collection of financial applications built on blockchain technology. These applications allow you to do things like earn interest, borrow funds, and trade assets—all without relying on traditional banks or intermediaries. But how does blockchain make this possible? Let's break it down.

Earn Interest: Lending and Yield Farming

One of the most popular use cases for DeFi is earning interest on your cryptocurrency. In traditional finance, you'd deposit your money in a bank and earn a small amount of interest. In DeFi, you can lend your crypto directly to others through decentralized lending platforms and earn significantly higher returns. How it works:

- You deposit your cryptocurrency into a DeFi lending platform (e.g., Aave or Compound).
- The platform uses smart contracts to match lenders with borrowers.
- Borrowers pay interest on their loans, and that interest is distributed to lenders.

Imagine you have 1 Ethereum (ETH) that you're not using. Instead of letting it sit idle, you could deposit it into a DeFi lending platform and earn interest—sometimes as high as 10% or more annually. This is far higher than the interest rates offered by traditional banks.

Yield Farming: For even higher returns, some users engage in yield farming, where they provide liquidity to decentralized exchanges (DEXs) and earn rewards in the form of additional cryptocurrency. While this can be more complex and risky, the potential rewards are substantial.

Borrow Funds: Collateralized Loans

Another key feature of DeFi is the ability to borrow funds using your cryptocurrency as collateral. This is particularly useful for those who want to access liquidity without selling their crypto holdings. How it works:

- You deposit cryptocurrency (e.g., ETH) as collateral into a DeFi lending platform.
- The platform allows you to borrow a percentage of the collateral's value in another cryptocurrency or stablecoin.
- You pay interest on the loan, and once it's repaid, your collateral is returned.

Let's say you own $10,000 worth of Bitcoin but don't want to sell it because you believe its value will increase. Instead, you could use it as collateral to borrow $5,000 in a stablecoin like USDC. You can then use that $5,000 for other investments or expenses, all while holding onto your Bitcoin.

Benefits:

- No credit checks or lengthy approval processes.
- Access to funds without selling your crypto.
- Lower interest rates compared to traditional loans.

Trade Assets: Decentralized Exchanges (DEXs)

In traditional finance, trading assets like stocks or currencies requires intermediaries like brokers or exchanges. In DeFi, you can trade directly with others using decentralized exchanges (DEXs). How it works:

- DEXs use smart contracts to facilitate peer-to-peer trading.
- Users connect their crypto wallets (e.g., MetaMask) to the DEX.
- Trades are executed automatically by smart contracts, with no need for a middleman.

Imagine you want to swap Ethereum (ETH) for Chainlink (LINK). On a DEX like Uniswap, you can do this in just a few clicks. The platform uses liquidity pools (funds provided by users) to facilitate the trade, and you pay a small fee for the service.

Benefits:

- No need to trust a centralized exchange with your funds.
- Lower fees compared to traditional exchanges.
- Access to a wide range of tokens, including new and emerging projects.

The Role of Smart Contracts and Cryptocurrency

At the heart of DeFi are smart contracts and cryptocurrencies, which work together to create a seamless, trustless financial ecosystem.

- *Smart Contracts:* These automate financial transactions, ensuring that agreements are executed exactly as programmed. For example, a lending platform's smart contract will automatically distribute interest to lenders and manage collateral for borrowers.
- *Cryptocurrencies:* These serve as the medium of exchange within DeFi. Whether you're lending, borrowing, or trading, cryptocurrencies are the assets that power these transactions.

Let's say you want to participate in a DeFi lending platform. You deposit your cryptocurrency into a smart contract, which then automatically matches you with a borrower. The borrower pays interest, and the smart contract distributes that interest to you—all without any human intervention.

Why Does This Matter?

Blockchain and cryptocurrency are more than just buzzwords—they're the building blocks of a new financial system. A system that's open to everyone, transparent, and free from the control of centralized institutions. Whether you're looking to grow your wealth, gain financial independence, or simply explore new opportunities, understanding these basics is the first step.

Blockchain technology enables DeFi by providing a secure, transparent, and trustless foundation for financial transactions. By eliminating intermediaries,

DeFi empowers individuals to take control of their finances, access new opportunities, and participate in a global financial system that's open to everyone.

Now that you've got the basics down, it's time to dive deeper into the world of DeFi. In the next chapter, we'll explore what DeFi is, how it works, and why it's such a game-changer. You'll learn about the key components of DeFi, from lending platforms to decentralized exchanges, and discover how you can start participating in this exciting new ecosystem.

So, are you ready to take the next step? Let's keep going—the decentralized future awaits!

Chapter 2: What is DeFi?

Imagine a financial system where you can earn interest on your savings, take out a loan, or trade assets—all without needing a bank, broker, or any other middleman. A system that's open to anyone, anywhere in the world, 24/7. This is the promise of *Decentralized Finance*, or *DeFi*. In this chapter, we'll explore what DeFi is, how it works, and why it's such a game-changer for the world of finance.

What is DeFi? A New Financial Paradigm

DeFi, short for Decentralized Finance, is a movement that aims to recreate traditional financial systems—like banking, lending, and trading—using blockchain technology. But it's not just a copy of the old system with a new coat of paint. DeFi represents a fundamental shift in how we think about money, trust, and financial services. Instead of relying on centralized institutions like banks, brokers, or payment processors, DeFi applications (often called dApps, or decentralized applications) operate on public blockchains like Ethereum. These applications are powered by smart contracts, which automate financial transactions and eliminate the need for intermediaries.

At its core, DeFi is about empowering individuals. It gives you control over your money, removes barriers to access, and opens up new opportunities for earning, borrowing, and investing. But to truly understand DeFi, we need to break it down into its core components and explore how it's changing the financial landscape.

The Problem with Traditional Finance

To appreciate the value of DeFi, it's important to understand the limitations of traditional finance. For decades, our financial systems have been dominated by centralized institutions—banks, credit card companies, stock exchanges, and governments. While these systems have enabled global economic growth, they come with significant drawbacks:

1. *High Fees:* Banks and payment processors charge fees for everything from wire transfers to currency conversions. These fees can add up, especially for international transactions.
2. *Slow Transactions:* Sending money across borders can take days, and even domestic transfers often require waiting periods.
3. *Limited Access:* Nearly 1.4 billion people worldwide are unbanked,

meaning they don't have access to basic financial services like savings accounts or loans. Even for those with bank accounts, services are often limited by geography, income, or credit history.

4. *Lack of Transparency:* Traditional financial systems are opaque. You have to trust that banks and institutions are handling your money correctly, but you can't see what's happening behind the scenes.
5. *Censorship and Control:* Governments and institutions can freeze accounts, block transactions, or impose restrictions on how you use your money.

How DeFi Solves These Problems

DeFi addresses these issues by leveraging blockchain technology to create a *decentralized, open, and transparent financial system*. Here's how:

1. *No Intermediaries:* DeFi eliminates the need for middlemen. Instead of relying on banks to facilitate transactions, DeFi uses smart contracts—self-executing agreements written in code—to automate financial processes. This reduces fees, speeds up transactions, and gives you full control over your money. **Example:** Imagine you want to send money to a friend in another country. With a traditional bank, you'd have to pay high fees, wait days for the transaction to clear, and trust the bank to handle it correctly. With DeFi, you can send cryptocurrency directly to your friend in minutes, with minimal fees, and without needing to trust a middleman.
2. *Global Access:* DeFi is open to anyone with an internet connection, regardless of where they live or their financial status. This is particularly powerful for the unbanked and underbanked populations, who can now access financial services for the first time. **Example:** A farmer in a remote village in Africa can use a DeFi lending platform to borrow funds for seeds and equipment, without needing a bank account or credit history.
3. *Transparency:* All transactions on DeFi platforms are recorded on a

public blockchain, making the system more transparent and trustworthy. You can see exactly how your money is being used and verify that the system is operating fairly. **Example:** On a DeFi lending platform, you can view the smart contract code to see how interest rates are calculated and how your funds are being managed.

4. *Censorship Resistance:* Because DeFi operates on decentralized networks, no single entity can control or shut it down. This makes it resistant to censorship and government interference. **Example:** In countries with strict capital controls, like Venezuela or Argentina, people have turned to DeFi to protect their wealth and access global financial markets.

The Building Blocks of DeFi

DeFi is built on a few key components that work together to create a seamless financial ecosystem:

1. *Blockchain Technology:* The foundation of DeFi is blockchain, a decentralized ledger that records transactions in a secure and transparent way.
2. *Smart Contracts:* These self-executing agreements automate financial transactions, eliminating the need for intermediaries. For example, a lending platform's smart contract can automatically distribute interest to lenders and manage collateral for borrowers.
3. *Cryptocurrencies:* Cryptocurrencies like Ethereum (ETH) and stablecoins like DAI are the native currencies of DeFi. They serve as the medium of exchange for transactions on DeFi platforms.
4. *Decentralized Applications (dApps):* These are the user-facing applications that allow you to interact with DeFi protocols. Examples include lending platforms like Aave, decentralized exchanges like Uniswap, and yield farming platforms like Yearn.finance.

DeFi is more than just a new way to manage money—it's a movement that's redefining the very nature of finance. By removing intermediaries, increasing transparency, and opening up access, DeFi has the potential to create a more inclusive and equitable financial system. Whether you're looking to earn interest, borrow funds, or trade assets, DeFi offers a world of possibilities.

Key DeFi Concepts: Lending, Borrowing, Trading, and Earning Interest

DeFi encompasses a wide range of financial activities, but most applications fall into a few key categories:

Lending and Borrowing: DeFi platforms allow you to lend your cryptocurrency and earn interest, or borrow funds using your crypto as collateral. This is all done through smart contracts, which automatically manage the terms of the loan.

Example: On platforms like *Aave* or *Compound*, you can deposit Ethereum (ETH) and earn interest, or borrow stablecoins like DAI by using your ETH as collateral.

Trading: Decentralized exchanges (DEXs) like *Uniswap* and *SushiSwap* let you trade cryptocurrencies directly with others, without needing a centralized exchange. These platforms use liquidity pools—funds provided by users—to facilitate trades.

Example: If you want to swap Bitcoin (BTC) for Chainlink (LINK), you can do so on Uniswap in just a few clicks, with no need for an intermediary.

Earning Interest: Beyond lending, DeFi offers other ways to earn passive income, such as yield farming and staking. Yield farming involves providing liquidity to DeFi protocols in exchange for rewards, while staking involves locking up your crypto to support a blockchain network and earning interest in return.

Example: On *Yearn.finance*, you can deposit stablecoins into a yield farming vault and earn high returns, often much higher than traditional savings accounts.

The Role of Ethereum and Other Blockchains in DeFi

While DeFi can technically be built on any blockchain, Ethereum is the undisputed leader in this space. Ethereum's support for smart contracts makes it the ideal platform for building complex financial applications. However, as the DeFi ecosystem grows, other blockchains like Binance Smart Chain (BSC), Solana, and Polygon are also gaining traction, offering faster transactions and lower fees. Let's explore why Ethereum dominates DeFi and how these alternative blockchains are carving out their own niches.

Why Ethereum? The Backbone of DeFi

Ethereum is often referred to as the "world computer" because of its ability to run decentralized applications (dApps) and smart contracts. Here's why it's the go-to platform for DeFi:

Smart Contracts: The Engine of DeFi

Smart contracts are self-executing agreements written in code. They automatically execute transactions when certain conditions are met, eliminating the need for intermediaries. Ethereum was the first blockchain to introduce smart contracts, and its robust programming language, Solidity, has become the standard for DeFi development.

When you deposit cryptocurrency into a DeFi lending platform like Aave, a smart contract automatically manages the loan, calculates interest, and distributes payments—all without human intervention.

Ecosystem: A Thriving Community

Ethereum has the largest and most active developer community in the blockchain space. This has led to a thriving ecosystem of DeFi projects, from lending platforms to decentralized exchanges. The sheer number of developers and users creates a network effect, making Ethereum the most secure and reliable platform for DeFi.

Popular DeFi protocols like Uniswap, Compound, and MakerDAO are all built on Ethereum. These projects have billions of dollars locked in their smart contracts, demonstrating the trust and confidence users have in the Ethereum ecosystem.

Interoperability: Seamless Integration

One of Ethereum's greatest strengths is its interoperability. Many DeFi protocols are designed to work together, creating a seamless experience for users. For example, you can borrow DAI (a stablecoin) from MakerDAO, use it to provide liquidity on Uniswap, and then stake your Uniswap tokens on Yearn.finance to earn additional rewards.

Example: Imagine you're a yield farmer. You start by depositing Ethereum (ETH) into Aave to earn interest. Then, you use the interest earned to provide liquidity on Uniswap, earning trading fees. Finally, you stake your Uniswap tokens on Yearn.finance to maximize your returns. All of this is possible because these protocols are built on Ethereum and designed to work together.

The Rise of Alternative Blockchains

While Ethereum is the leader in DeFi, it's not without its challenges. High gas fees (transaction costs) and network congestion have led developers and users to explore alternative blockchains. Here are a few of the most prominent ones:

Binance Smart Chain (BSC): Speed and Affordability

Binance Smart Chain is a blockchain developed by the cryptocurrency exchange Binance. It's designed to be compatible with Ethereum, meaning developers can easily port their dApps from Ethereum to BSC. BSC offers faster transactions and lower fees, making it an attractive option for users.

PancakeSwap, a popular decentralized exchange, is built on BSC. It offers similar functionality to Uniswap but with much lower transaction costs, making it a favorite among small-scale traders and yield farmers.

Solana: High-Speed and Scalability

Solana is a high-performance blockchain designed for scalability. It can process thousands of transactions per second (TPS) with minimal fees, making it ideal for DeFi applications that require speed and efficiency.

Serum, a decentralized exchange built on Solana, offers lightning-fast trades and low fees, attracting users who want to avoid the high costs and slow speeds of Ethereum.

Polygon: Ethereum's Scaling Solution

Polygon (formerly Matic) is a layer-2 scaling solution for Ethereum. It aims to address Ethereum's scalability issues by processing transactions off-chain and then settling them on the Ethereum mainnet. This reduces congestion and lowers fees while maintaining Ethereum's security.

Aave has a version of its lending platform on Polygon, allowing users to borrow and lend cryptocurrencies with much lower fees than on Ethereum.

Overview of DeFi Protocols

DeFi is powered by a growing number of protocols, each offering unique features and services. These protocols are the building blocks of the DeFi ecosystem, enabling everything from lending and borrowing to trading and yield farming. Here's a closer look at some of the most popular DeFi protocols and how they're shaping the future of finance.

1. Aave: Decentralized Lending and Borrowing

Aave is a decentralized lending platform that allows users to lend and borrow a wide range of cryptocurrencies. It's one of the most popular DeFi protocols, with billions of dollars locked in its smart contracts.

- *Lending:* Users deposit cryptocurrency into Aave's liquidity pools and earn interest. The interest rates are dynamic, meaning they fluctuate based on supply and demand.
- *Borrowing:* Users can borrow cryptocurrency by providing collateral. The amount they can borrow depends on the collateral's value and the platform's loan-to-value (LTV) ratio.

Unique Features:

- *Flash Loans:* Aave pioneered the concept of flash loans, which allow users to borrow funds without collateral as long as the loan is repaid within the same transaction. This is particularly useful for arbitrage and other advanced strategies.
- *aTokens:* When you deposit funds into Aave, you receive aTokens in return. These tokens accrue interest in real-time, making it easy to track your earnings.

Example: Imagine you have 10 Ethereum (ETH) that you're not using. You can deposit it into Aave and earn interest. If you need cash, you can borrow stablecoins like DAI or USDC using your ETH as collateral.

2. Uniswap: Decentralized Trading

Uniswap is a decentralized exchange (DEX) that allows users to trade cryptocurrencies directly with each other. It's one of the most widely used DEXs, known for its simplicity and liquidity.

- *Liquidity Pools:* Instead of using an order book like traditional exchanges, Uniswap uses liquidity pools. Users (called liquidity providers) deposit pairs of tokens (e.g., ETH and DAI) into these pools, and traders can swap tokens directly from the pool.
- *Automated Market Making (AMM):* Uniswap uses an AMM model to determine prices. The price of a token is based on the ratio of tokens in the pool, and it adjusts automatically as trades are executed.

Unique Features:

- *Permissionless Listing:* Anyone can list a token on Uniswap by creating a liquidity pool. This has made it a popular platform for new and emerging projects.
- *UNI Token:* Uniswap's native token, UNI, is used for governance. Holders can vote on proposals to shape the future of the protocol.

Example: If you want to swap Ethereum (ETH) for Chainlink (LINK), you can do so on Uniswap in just a few clicks. The platform uses liquidity pools to facilitate the trade, and you pay a small fee for the service.

3. Compound: Earn Interest on Your Crypto

Compound is a decentralized lending protocol that allows users to earn interest on their cryptocurrency deposits or borrow funds using crypto as collateral.

- *Lending:* Users deposit cryptocurrency into Compound's liquidity pools and earn interest. The interest rates are algorithmically adjusted based on supply and demand.
- *Borrowing:* Users can borrow cryptocurrency by providing collateral. The amount they can borrow depends on the collateral's value and the platform's collateral factor.

Unique Features:

- *cTokens:* When you deposit funds into Compound, you receive cTokens in return. These tokens represent your share of the liquidity pool and accrue interest over time.
- *Governance:* Compound has a decentralized governance model, where COMP token holders can vote on proposals to change the protocol.

Example: Let's say you deposit 1 Bitcoin (BTC) into Compound. You'll receive cBTC tokens, which accrue interest. If you need cash, you can borrow stablecoins like USDC using your BTC as collateral.

4. Yearn.finance: Automated Yield Farming

Yearn.finance is an automated yield farming platform that helps users maximize their returns by automatically moving their funds between different DeFi protocols.

- *Vaults:* Users deposit cryptocurrency into Yearn's vaults, and the platform automatically allocates the funds to the highest-yielding DeFi strategies.
- *Strategies:* Yearn's strategies include lending on Aave, providing liquidity on Uniswap, and staking on Curve Finance. The platform constantly monitors the market and reallocates funds to maximize returns.

Unique Features:

- *Automation:* Yearn takes the guesswork out of yield farming by automating the process. Users don't need to constantly monitor the market or manually move their funds.
- *yTokens:* When you deposit funds into a Yearn vault, you receive yTokens in return. These tokens represent your share of the vault and accrue interest over time.

Example: Imagine you have $10,000 in stablecoins. Instead of manually searching for the best yield farming opportunities, you can deposit your funds into a Yearn vault and let the platform do the work for you.

5. MakerDAO: Decentralized Credit and Stablecoins

MakerDAO is a decentralized credit platform that issues the DAI stablecoin. DAI is pegged to the US dollar and is one of the most widely used stablecoins in DeFi.

- *Collateralized Debt Positions (CDPs):* Users lock up cryptocurrency (like ETH) as collateral and mint DAI in return. The amount of DAI they can mint depends on the collateral's value and the platform's collateralization ratio.
- *Stability Mechanism:* DAI maintains its peg to the US dollar through a combination of collateralization, interest rates, and governance.

Unique Features:

- *Decentralized Governance:* MakerDAO is governed by MKR token holders, who vote on proposals to change the protocol.
- *Multi-Collateral DAI:* Initially, DAI was backed only by ETH, but it now supports multiple types of collateral, including BAT and USDC.

Example: Let's say you have 10 Ethereum (ETH) and need cash. You can lock up your ETH in a MakerDAO CDP and mint 5,000 DAI. You can then use the DAI for other DeFi activities, like providing liquidity on Uniswap or earning interest on Aave.

These protocols are just the tip of the iceberg—there are hundreds of DeFi projects, each contributing to the ecosystem in its own way. From insurance platforms like *Nexus Mutual* to prediction markets like *Augur*, the possibilities are endless. As the DeFi space continues to grow, we can expect even more innovation and opportunities for users.

The DeFi Ecosystem

To help you visualize how all these components fit together, here's a simplified diagram of the DeFi ecosystem:

```
[Blockchain Layer (e.g., Ethereum)]
       |
       v
[Smart Contracts (e.g., Aave, Uniswap)]
       |
       v
[DeFi Applications (e.g., Lending, Trading, Yield Farming)]
       |
       v
[Users (Lenders, Borrowers, Traders, Yield Farmers)]
```

This diagram shows how blockchain technology enables smart contracts, which in turn power DeFi applications that serve users around the world.

Why DeFi Matters

DeFi is more than just a new way to manage money—it's a movement that's redefining the very nature of finance. By removing intermediaries, increasing transparency, and opening up access, DeFi has the potential to create a more inclusive and equitable financial system. Whether you're looking to earn interest, borrow funds, or trade assets, DeFi offers a world of possibilities.

In the next chapter, we'll dive into how to get started with DeFi, providing step-by-step guidance on setting up a wallet, buying cryptocurrency, and connecting to DeFi platforms. So, let's keep going—the decentralized future is waiting for you!

Chapter 3: How to Get Started with DeFi

So, you've heard about the incredible opportunities in *Decentralized Finance (DeFi)*—earning interest on your crypto, borrowing funds, trading assets, and more. But how do you actually get started? If you're new to DeFi, the process might seem a bit overwhelming at first. Don't worry—this chapter will walk you through everything you need to know, step by step. By the end, you'll be ready to dive into the world of DeFi with confidence.

Step 1: Setting Up a Crypto Wallet

Before you can start using DeFi, you'll need a *crypto wallet*. Think of this as your gateway to the decentralized world. A crypto wallet is a digital tool that allows you to store, send, and receive cryptocurrencies. More importantly, it lets you interact with DeFi platforms.

Why You Need a Wallet:

Unlike traditional finance, where banks hold your money, DeFi gives you full control over your funds. Your wallet is where you'll store your cryptocurrency and manage your transactions.

Recommended Wallet: MetaMask

MetaMask is one of the most popular crypto wallets for DeFi. It's easy to use, supports Ethereum and other compatible blockchains, and integrates seamlessly with most DeFi platforms.

How to Set Up MetaMask:

1. Download the App: Go to the MetaMask website (https://metamask.io) and download the app for your browser or mobile device.
2. Create a Wallet: Follow the prompts to create a new wallet. Make sure to write down your seed phrase (a series of 12 words) and store it in a safe place. This is your backup in case you lose access to your wallet.
3. Secure Your Wallet: Set a strong password and enable two-factor authentication (2FA) if available.
4. Add Funds: Once your wallet is set up, you'll need to add cryptocurrency (like Ethereum) to start using DeFi.

Additional Tips:

- Browser Extension: If you're using MetaMask on a desktop, install the browser extension for easy access.
- Mobile App: For on-the-go access, download the MetaMask mobile app.
- Backup Your Seed Phrase: Store your seed phrase in multiple secure locations (e.g., a safe, a password manager). Never share it with anyone.

Step 2: Acquiring Cryptocurrency

To participate in DeFi, you'll need cryptocurrency—specifically, *Ethereum (ETH)* or other tokens supported by DeFi platforms. Here's how to get started:

Option 1: Buy Crypto on a Centralized Exchange

Centralized exchanges like Coinbase, Binance, or Kraken are the easiest way to buy cryptocurrency. Here's how:

1. *Create an Account:* Sign up for an account on the exchange and complete the verification process.
2. *Deposit Funds:* Link your bank account or credit card to deposit fiat currency (like USD or EUR).
3. *Buy Crypto:* Purchase Ethereum (ETH) or another supported cryptocurrency.
4. *Transfer to Your Wallet:* Withdraw your crypto from the exchange and send it to your MetaMask wallet.

Option 2: Use a Peer-to-Peer (P2P) Platform

If you prefer a more decentralized approach, you can buy crypto directly from other individuals using P2P platforms like *LocalBitcoins* or *Paxful.*

- *Start Small:* Begin with a small amount of cryptocurrency to familiarize yourself with the process. You can always buy more later.
- *Check Fees:* Compare fees across different exchanges to get the best deal.
- *Secure Your Exchange Account:* Enable 2FA and use a strong, unique password for your exchange account.

Step 3: Connecting Your Wallet to DeFi Platforms

Now that you have a wallet and some cryptocurrency, it's time to connect to DeFi platforms. Here's how:

1. *Choose a DeFi Platform:* Start with a popular platform like *Aave* (for lending), *Uniswap* (for trading), or *Compound* (for earning interest).
2. *Connect Your Wallet:* On the platform's website, look for a button that says "Connect Wallet" or something similar. Select MetaMask and follow the prompts to connect.
3. *Authorize Transactions:* When you perform an action (like depositing funds or swapping tokens), MetaMask will pop up asking you to confirm the transaction. Review the details and confirm.

Let's say you want to lend your Ethereum on Aave. After connecting your wallet, you'll deposit your ETH into Aave's liquidity pool. MetaMask will ask you to confirm the transaction, and once it's processed, you'll start earning interest.

Additional Tips:

- *Bookmark Trusted Sites:* Always access DeFi platforms through official websites or trusted links to avoid phishing scams.
- *Double-Check Addresses:* When sending or receiving crypto, double-check wallet addresses to ensure they're correct.
- *Use Hardware Wallets:* For added security, consider using a hardware wallet like Ledger or Trezor in conjunction with MetaMask.

Step 4: Understanding Gas Fees and Transaction Costs

One of the most important things to understand when using DeFi is *gas fees*. Gas fees are the costs associated with processing transactions on the blockchain. They're paid in cryptocurrency (usually ETH) and can vary depending on network congestion.

What Are Gas Fees?

Every transaction on the Ethereum network (and other blockchains) requires computational resources. Gas fees compensate miners or validators for processing these transactions.

How to Manage Gas Fees:

- Check Gas Prices: Use tools like *Etherscan* or *GasNow* to check current gas prices before making a transaction.
- Adjust Gas Limits: When confirming a transaction in MetaMask, you can adjust the gas limit and gas price. Higher gas prices mean faster transactions, but they also cost more.
- Time Your Transactions: Gas fees tend to be lower during off-peak hours (e.g., late at night or early in the morning).

Example: If you're swapping tokens on Uniswap, you might see a gas fee of 10–10–20 during peak times. If you're not in a hurry, you can wait for fees to drop before confirming the transaction.

Additional Tips:

- Use Layer 2 Solutions: Consider using Layer 2 solutions like *Polygon* or *Optimism* to reduce gas fees.
- Batch Transactions: If possible, batch multiple transactions into one to

save on gas fees.

- Stay Informed: Follow Ethereum network updates to stay informed about changes that could affect gas fees.

Checklist for Setting Up a Wallet and Buying Crypto

To make sure you're ready to start using DeFi, here's a quick checklist:

Set Up MetaMask:

- Download and install MetaMask.
- Create a wallet and securely store your seed phrase.
- Set a strong password and enable 2FA if available.

Buy Cryptocurrency:

- Sign up for a centralized exchange (e.g., Coinbase, Binance).
- Deposit fiat currency and buy Ethereum (ETH).
- Transfer your ETH to your MetaMask wallet.

Connect to DeFi:

- Choose a DeFi platform (e.g., Aave, Uniswap).
- Connect your MetaMask wallet.
- Start exploring (e.g., deposit funds, swap tokens).

Understand Gas Fees:

- Check gas prices before making transactions.
- Adjust gas limits and prices as needed.
- Time your transactions to save on fees.

Why This Matters

Getting started with DeFi might seem like a lot of steps, but it's worth the effort. By taking control of your finances and participating in the decentralized economy, you're joining a movement that's redefining the future of money. Whether you're looking to earn interest, borrow funds, or trade assets, DeFi offers a world of possibilities—and it all starts with setting up a wallet and acquiring some cryptocurrency.

In the next chapter, we'll dive into earning passive income with DeFi, exploring strategies like yield farming, staking, and liquidity mining. So, let's keep going—the decentralized future is waiting for you!

Chapter 4: Earning Passive Income with DeFi

Now that you've set up your wallet, acquired some cryptocurrency, and connected to DeFi platforms, it's time to explore one of the most exciting aspects of decentralized finance: earning passive income. Unlike traditional savings accounts that offer meager interest rates, DeFi allows you to earn substantial returns on your crypto holdings. In this chapter, we'll dive into the most popular ways to earn passive income in DeFi, including *lending, yield farming, staking, and liquidity mining.* By the end, you'll have a clear understanding of how to put your crypto to work and start earning.

1. Lending: Earn Interest on Your Crypto

One of the simplest ways to earn passive income in DeFi is by lending your cryptocurrency. DeFi lending platforms like Aave and Compound allow you to deposit your crypto into liquidity pools and earn interest in return. How it works:

- *Deposit Your Crypto:* You deposit cryptocurrency (e.g., Ethereum, stablecoins) into a lending platform.
- *Earn Interest:* Borrowers pay interest on their loans, and that interest is distributed to lenders.
- *Withdraw Anytime:* You can withdraw your funds (plus interest) at any

time.

Example: Let's say you deposit 1 Ethereum (ETH) into Aave. Depending on market conditions, you might earn an annual interest rate of 5–10%. Over time, your ETH balance will grow as you earn interest.

Benefits:

- Low Risk: Lending is one of the lower-risk ways to earn passive income in DeFi.
- Flexibility: You can withdraw your funds at any time.
- Compound Interest: Some platforms automatically reinvest your earnings, allowing you to earn interest on your interest.

Tips for Success:

- Diversify: Spread your funds across multiple platforms to reduce risk.
- Monitor Rates: Interest rates can fluctuate, so keep an eye on them to maximize your returns.
- Use Stablecoins: For more stable returns, consider lending stablecoins like DAI or USDC.

2. Yield Farming: Maximize Your Returns

Yield farming is a more advanced strategy that involves providing liquidity to DeFi protocols in exchange for rewards. These rewards can come in the form of interest, trading fees, or additional tokens. How it works:

- *Provide Liquidity:* You deposit cryptocurrency into a liquidity pool on a decentralized exchange (DEX) like Uniswap or SushiSwap.
- *Earn Rewards:* In return, you earn a share of the trading fees generated by

the pool, as well as additional tokens (often called yield farming rewards).

- *Compound Your Earnings:* You can reinvest your rewards to maximize your returns.

Example: Imagine you deposit 1,000 worth of Ethereum(ETH) and 1,000 worth of DAI into a liquidity pool on Uniswap. You'll earn a share of the trading fees generated by the pool, as well as UNI tokens (Uniswap's native token) as additional rewards.

Benefits:

- High Returns: Yield farming can offer much higher returns than traditional lending.
- Diverse Opportunities: There are countless yield farming opportunities across different platforms and tokens.

Risks:

- *Impermanent Loss:* If the price of the tokens in your liquidity pool changes significantly, you could experience impermanent loss.
- *Smart Contract Risk:* Yield farming involves interacting with complex smart contracts, which could have vulnerabilities.

Tips for Success:

- Start Small: Begin with a small amount of capital to familiarize yourself with the process.
- Research Platforms: Choose reputable platforms with a track record of security and reliability.
- Diversify: Spread your funds across multiple pools to reduce risk.

3. Staking: Earn Rewards for Supporting the Network

Staking is another popular way to earn passive income in DeFi. It involves locking up your cryptocurrency to support a blockchain network and earn rewards in return. How it works:

- *Lock Up Your Crypto:* You lock up your cryptocurrency in a staking pool or validator node.
- *Earn Rewards:* In return, you earn staking rewards, which are typically paid in the same cryptocurrency you staked.
- *Unlock Your Funds:* Depending on the platform, you may need to wait a certain period before you can withdraw your staked funds.

Example: Let's say you stake 10 Ethereum (ETH) on a staking platform like Lido or Rocket Pool. You might earn an annual return of 4–7%, paid in ETH.

Benefits:

- Support the Network: Staking helps secure and decentralize the blockchain network.
- Predictable Returns: Staking rewards are often more predictable than yield farming returns.
- Low Maintenance: Once you've staked your crypto, you don't need to do much else to earn rewards.

Risks:

- Lock-Up Periods: Some staking platforms require you to lock up your funds for a certain period.
- Slashing: If the validator node you're staking with behaves maliciously, you could lose a portion of your staked funds.

Tips for Success:

- Choose Reputable Platforms: Stick to well-known staking platforms with a strong track record.
- Diversify: Consider staking multiple cryptocurrencies to spread your risk.
- Monitor Performance: Keep an eye on the performance of your staking pool or validator node.

4. Liquidity Mining: Earn Tokens for Providing Liquidity

Liquidity mining is similar to yield farming but focuses specifically on earning tokens for providing liquidity to DeFi platforms. These tokens can often be traded or staked for additional rewards. How it works:

- *Provide Liquidity:* You deposit cryptocurrency into a liquidity pool on a DeFi platform.
- *Earn Tokens:* In return, you earn the platform's native tokens as rewards.
- *Reinvest or Trade:* You can reinvest your tokens to earn more rewards or trade them for other cryptocurrencies.

Example: Let's say you provide liquidity to a pool on *Curve Finance.* In return, you earn CRV tokens, which you can then stake to earn additional rewards.

Benefits:

- High Potential Returns: Liquidity mining can offer very high returns, especially in the early stages of a project.
- Diverse Opportunities: There are countless liquidity mining opportunities across different platforms and tokens.

Risks:

- Token Volatility: The value of the tokens you earn can be highly volatile.
- Impermanent Loss: As with yield farming, you could experience impermanent loss if the price of the tokens in your pool changes significantly.

Tips for Success:

- Research Projects: Choose projects with strong fundamentals and a clear use case for their tokens.
- Diversify: Spread your funds across multiple liquidity pools to reduce risk.
- Monitor Performance: Keep an eye on the performance of your liquidity pools and adjust your strategy as needed.

Actionable Tip: Start Small and Diversify

When it comes to earning passive income in DeFi, one of the most important principles to follow is to start small and diversify. The decentralized finance space is full of opportunities, but it's also fraught with risks—smart contract vulnerabilities, market volatility, and impermanent loss, to name a few. By starting small and spreading your investments across multiple platforms and strategies, you can minimize your risk while maximizing your potential returns. Let's break this down further.

Why Starting Small Matters

DeFi is an exciting and rapidly evolving space, but it's also complex and can be overwhelming for newcomers. Here's why starting small is crucial:

Learn the Ropes:

DeFi platforms and protocols can be tricky to navigate, especially if you're new to blockchain technology. By starting with a small amount of capital, you can learn how these platforms work without risking significant losses.

Example: Instead of depositing $10,000 into a yield farming pool right start with $100 or $500. This allows you to understand how the process works, monitor your returns, and identify any potential pitfalls.

Test the Waters:

Not all DeFi platforms are created equal. Some are more user-friendly, while others are more complex. By starting small, you can test different platforms and strategies to see which ones work best for you.

Example: Try lending a small amount of Ethereum on Aave and providing liquidity to a stablecoin pool on Uniswap. Compare the returns, risks, and user experience to determine which strategy suits your goals.

Manage Risk:

DeFi is inherently risky, and even the most reputable platforms can experience issues like smart contract bugs or market crashes. By starting small, you limit your exposure to these risks while still participating in the ecosystem.

Example: If you lose $100 due to impermanent loss or a sudden market downturn, it's a valuable learning experience. Losing $10,000, on the other hand, could be devastating.

The Power of Diversification

Diversification is a key strategy in any investment portfolio, and it's especially important in DeFi. Here's why:

Spread Your Risk:

By spreading your funds across multiple platforms and strategies, you reduce the impact of any single failure. If one platform experiences issues or one strategy underperforms, your overall portfolio will be less affected.

Example: Instead of putting all your funds into a single yield farming pool, consider splitting them between lending on Compound, staking on Lido, and providing liquidity on Curve Finance.

Maximize Returns:

Different DeFi platforms and strategies offer varying levels of risk and reward. By diversifying, you can balance high-risk, high-reward opportunities (like yield farming) with lower-risk, steady returns (like lending).

Example: Allocate 50% of your funds to low-risk lending, 30% to medium-risk staking, and 20% to high-risk yield farming. This way, you can enjoy steady returns while still participating in more lucrative opportunities.

Explore New Opportunities:

The DeFi space is constantly evolving, with new platforms and protocols launching regularly. By diversifying, you can explore these new opportunities without putting all your eggs in one basket.

Example: If a new DeFi platform launches with an attractive yield farming program, you can allocate a small portion of your funds to test it out without risking your entire portfolio.

How to Diversify Effectively

Diversification isn't just about spreading your funds randomly—it's about creating a balanced portfolio that aligns with your risk tolerance and financial goals. Here's how to do it effectively:

Allocate by Risk Level:

Divide your funds into low-risk, medium-risk, and high-risk categories. For example:

- *Low-Risk:* Lending on platforms like Aave or Compound.
- *Medium-Risk:* Staking on platforms like Lido or Rocket Pool.
- *High-Risk:* Yield farming or liquidity mining on platforms like Uniswap or SushiSwap.

Choose Reputable Platforms:

Stick to well-established platforms with a strong track record of security and reliability. Avoid new or untested platforms unless you're willing to take on additional risk.

Monitor and Adjust:

Regularly review your portfolio to ensure it's performing as expected. If one strategy is underperforming or a platform is experiencing issues, reallocate your funds accordingly.

Example: If the returns on a yield farming pool drop significantly, consider moving your funds to a different pool or strategy.

Stay Informed:

The DeFi space moves quickly, with new opportunities and risks emerging all the time. Stay informed by following industry news, joining DeFi communities, and participating in governance discussions.

A Diversified DeFi Portfolio

Let's say you have $5,000 to invest in DeFi. Here's how you might diversify your portfolio:

- *Lending (Low-Risk):* $2,000 Deposit, $1,000 in Ethereum on Aave and $1,000 in stablecoins on Compound. This provides steady returns with minimal risk.
- *Staking (Medium-Risk):* $1,500 Stake, $1,000 in Ethereum on Lido and $500 in a promising altcoin on a staking platform like Kraken. This offers higher returns with moderate risk.
- *Yield Farming (High-Risk):* $1,500 Provide liquidity to a stable coin pool on *Uniswap* ($1,000) and a high-yield farming pool on *SushiSwap* ($500). This offers the potential for high returns but comes with higher risk.

By diversifying in this way, you balance risk and reward while taking advantage of the full range of opportunities in DeFi.

Why This Matters

Earning passive income in DeFi is one of the most exciting aspects of decentralized finance. Whether you're lending your crypto, providing liquidity, or staking your tokens, DeFi offers a world of opportunities to grow your wealth. By understanding the different strategies and managing your risk, you can take full advantage of these opportunities and start earning passive income today.

In the next chapter, we'll explore borrowing and lending in DeFi, diving deeper into how you can use your crypto as collateral to access loans and other financial services. So, let's keep going—the decentralized future is waiting for you!

Chapter 5: Borrowing and Lending in DeFi

One of the most transformative aspects of Decentralized Finance (DeFi) is its ability to revolutionize the way we borrow and lend money. In traditional finance, borrowing and lending are dominated by banks and other centralized institutions, which often impose high fees, strict eligibility criteria, and lengthy approval processes. DeFi flips this model on its head, allowing anyone with an internet connection and some cryptocurrency to participate in a global, open, and transparent financial system. In this chapter, we'll explore how borrowing and lending work in DeFi, the benefits and risks involved, and how you can get started.

How Borrowing and Lending Work in DeFi

At its core, DeFi borrowing and lending operate through smart contracts, which automate the process and eliminate the need for intermediaries. Here's how it works:

- *Lending:* Users deposit cryptocurrency into a lending platform's liquidity pool. In return, they earn interest on their deposits. The interest rates are typically higher than those offered by traditional banks and are determined algorithmically based on supply and demand.
- *Borrowing:* Users can borrow cryptocurrency by providing collateral.

The amount they can borrow depends on the value of the collateral and the platform's loan-to-value (LTV) ratio. Borrowers pay interest on their loans, which is distributed to lenders.

Example: Let's say you deposit 10 Ethereum (ETH) into Aave. You start earning interest on your deposit. If you need cash, you can borrow $5,000 worth of DAI (a stablecoin) by using your ETH as collateral. You'll pay interest on the loan, but you can repay it at any time to reclaim your collateral.

- *Interest Rates:* Interest rates in DeFi are often variable and can change based on market conditions. Some platforms offer both stable and variable rates, giving users more flexibility.
- *Collateralization:* Most DeFi platforms require over-collateralization, meaning you need to deposit more collateral than the amount you wish to borrow. This protects the platform from price volatility.
- *Liquidation:* If the value of your collateral drops below a certain threshold, your position may be liquidated to repay the loan. This is a critical risk to manage.

Key Benefits of DeFi Borrowing and Lending

DeFi borrowing and lending offer several advantages over traditional finance:

1. *No Intermediaries:* DeFi eliminates the need for banks and other intermediaries, reducing fees and speeding up transactions. This also means no credit checks or lengthy approval processes.
2. *Global Access:* Anyone with an internet connection and some cryptocurrency can participate, regardless of their location or financial status. This is particularly empowering for people in underbanked regions.
3. *Transparency:* All transactions are recorded on a public blockchain, making the system more transparent and trustworthy. You can verify

every transaction and see exactly how your funds are being used.

4. *Flexibility:* You can borrow and lend a wide range of cryptocurrencies, and you're not limited by traditional banking hours or processes. This flexibility allows for more dynamic financial management.
5. *Higher Returns:* Interest rates on DeFi lending platforms are often significantly higher than those offered by traditional banks. This makes DeFi an attractive option for earning passive income.

Example: In traditional finance, a savings account might offer an annual interest rate of 0.5%. In DeFi, you could earn 5–10% or more by lending stablecoins like DAI or USDC.

Popular DeFi Lending Platforms

Here are some of the most popular DeFi lending platforms:

1. *Aave:* Aave is a decentralized lending platform that allows users to lend and borrow a wide range of cryptocurrencies. It's known for its innovative features, such as flash loans and aTokens.
2. *Compound:* Compound is another popular lending platform that allows users to earn interest on their crypto deposits or borrow funds using crypto as collateral. It uses cTokens to represent users' shares of the liquidity pool.
3. *MakerDAO:* MakerDAO is a decentralized credit platform that issues the DAI stablecoin. Users can lock up collateral (like ETH) in a Collateralized Debt Position (CDP) and mint DAI in return.
4. *Cream Finance:* Cream Finance is a decentralized lending platform that supports a wide range of assets, including cryptocurrencies and tokenized stocks.

Additional Details:

- *Flash Loans:* Aave's flash loans allow users to borrow funds without collateral as long as the loan is repaid within the same transaction. This is particularly useful for arbitrage and other advanced strategies.
- *Governance Tokens:* Many DeFi platforms, like Compound and Aave, have their own governance tokens (COMP and AAVE, respectively). These tokens allow users to participate in the platform's governance and earn additional rewards.

How to Get Started with DeFi Borrowing and Lending

Ready to start borrowing and lending in DeFi? Here's a step-by-step guide:

1. *Set Up a Crypto Wallet:* If you haven't already, set up a crypto wallet like MetaMask and fund it with cryptocurrency.
2. *Choose a Lending Platform:* Select a reputable lending platform like Aave or Compound.
3. *Connect Your Wallet:* Connect your wallet to the lending platform by clicking the "Connect Wallet" button and following the prompts.
4. *Deposit Funds:* Deposit cryptocurrency into the platform's liquidity pool. You'll start earning interest on your deposit.
5. *Borrow Funds (Optional):* If you need to borrow funds, provide collateral and specify the amount you want to borrow. Be sure to understand the platform's LTV ratio and interest rates.
6. *Monitor Your Position:* Keep an eye on your deposits, loans, and interest rates. If the value of your collateral drops significantly, you may need to add more collateral or repay part of your loan to avoid liquidation.

Understanding Risks

While DeFi borrowing and lending offer many benefits, they also come with risks:

1. *Smart Contract Risk:* DeFi platforms rely on smart contracts, which can have vulnerabilities. If a smart contract is hacked or exploited, you could lose your funds.
2. *Market Volatility:* The value of your collateral can fluctuate significantly, especially if it's a volatile asset like Ethereum. If the value drops too much, your collateral could be liquidated.
3. *Liquidation Risk:* If the value of your collateral falls below a certain threshold (the LTV ratio), your position may be liquidated, and you could lose your collateral.
4. *Regulatory Risk:* The regulatory environment for DeFi is still evolving, and new regulations could impact the availability or legality of certain platforms and services.

Example: During a market crash, the value of your ETH collateral could drop rapidly, triggering a liquidation. To avoid this, you might need to add more collateral or repay part of your loan.

The Bigger Picture: A Financial Revolution in the Making

DeFi borrowing and lending are more than just new ways to manage money—they're part of a broader movement to create a more open, transparent, and inclusive financial system. By removing intermediaries, increasing transparency, and opening up access, DeFi is empowering individuals to take control of their finances and participate in a global economy.

Imagine a small business owner in a developing country who needs a loan to expand their business. In the traditional system, they might be denied due to lack of credit history or high fees. With DeFi, they can use their crypto as collateral to access the funds they need, all while earning interest on their deposits.

As we move forward in this book, we'll explore decentralized exchanges (DEXs), diving into how they work, the benefits they offer, and how you can start trading on them. So, let's keep going—the decentralized future is waiting for you!

Chapter 6: Decentralized Exchanges (DEXs)

In the world of traditional finance, trading assets like stocks, currencies, or commodities requires intermediaries such as brokers, exchanges, and clearinghouses. These middlemen not only add layers of complexity and cost but also control access to the markets. Decentralized Exchanges (DEXs) are changing this paradigm by enabling peer-to-peer trading directly on the blockchain, without the need for intermediaries. In this chapter, we'll explore how DEXs work, their advantages over centralized exchanges, and how you can start trading on them. By the end, you'll understand why DEXs are a cornerstone of the DeFi ecosystem and how to use them to trade assets securely and efficiently.

What Are Decentralized Exchanges (DEXs)?

A **Decentralized Exchange (DEX)** is a platform that allows users to trade cryptocurrencies directly with one another, without relying on a central authority to facilitate transactions. Instead of using an order book like traditional exchanges, most DEXs use Automated Market Makers (AMMs) and liquidity pools to enable trading. Key features of DEXs:

- *No Intermediaries:* Trades are executed directly between users through smart contracts.

- *Non-Custodial:* You retain control of your funds at all times; the exchange never holds them.
- *Permissionless:* Anyone with a crypto wallet can trade, regardless of location or identity.
- *Transparency:* All transactions are recorded on the blockchain, making them publicly verifiable.

Example: On Uniswap, one of the most popular DEXs, you can swap Ethereum (ETH) for Chainlink (LINK) directly from your wallet, without needing to create an account or go through a centralized exchange.

How DEXs Work: The Role of Liquidity Pools and AMMs

Liquidity Pools: The Backbone of DEXs

Liquidity pools are essentially pools of tokens locked in a smart contract. These pools are created and maintained by *liquidity providers (LPs),* who deposit pairs of tokens (e.g., ETH and DAI) into the pool. In return, they earn a share of the trading fees generated by the pool. How Liquidity Pools work:

1. *Token Pairs:* Liquidity pools consist of pairs of tokens, such as ETH/DAI or BTC/USDC. These pairs enable users to trade one token for another directly from the pool.
2. *Liquidity Providers (LPs):* Users who deposit tokens into the pool are called liquidity providers. They contribute equal value of both tokens in the pair to maintain the pool's balance.
3. *Trading Fees:* Every time a trade occurs, a small fee (usually 0.3% on platforms like Uniswap) is charged and distributed to the liquidity providers as a reward.

Example: If you deposit 1 ETH and 3,000 DAI into an ETH/DAI liquidity pool on Uniswap, you're providing liquidity for others to trade ETH for DAI and vice versa. In return, you earn a share of the trading fees.

Why Liquidity Pools Matter: Liquidity pools are the foundation of DEXs because they provide the necessary liquidity for trading. Without them, users would have to rely on finding a counterparty to trade with, which could be slow and inefficient.

Automated Market Makers (AMMs): The Engine of DEXs

Automated Market Makers (AMMs) are algorithms that determine the price of tokens in a liquidity pool based on the ratio of tokens in the pool. Unlike traditional exchanges, where prices are determined by buyers and sellers, AMMs use a mathematical formula to set prices automatically. How AMMs work:

Constant Product Formula: Most AMMs, including Uniswap, use the constant product formula:

$$x \times y = kx \times y = k$$

Here, xx and yy represent the quantities of the two tokens in the pool, and kk is a constant. The product of the two token quantities must always remain the same, which means that as one token is bought, its price increases, and the other token's price decreases.

Price Determination: The price of a token is determined by the ratio of the two tokens in the pool. For example, if a pool has 10 ETH and 30,000 DAI, the price of ETH in terms of DAI is 3,000 DAI per ETH.

Slippage: Slippage occurs when the price of a token changes between the time you initiate a trade and the time it's executed. Larger trades can cause more significant price changes due to the constant product formula.

Example: Let's say you want to swap 1 ETH for DAI in a pool that has 10

ETH and 30,000 DAI. According to the constant product formula:

$$10\times30{,}000=300{,}000$$

After your trade, the pool will have 11 ETH and 300,000/11=27,272.73 DAI. This means you'll receive 30,000 - 27,272.73 = 2,727.27 DAI for your 1 ETH. The price of ETH in the pool has now increased to approximately 2,727 DAI per ETH.

The Role of Liquidity Providers (LPs)

Liquidity providers play a crucial role in the functioning of DEXs. Here's what you need to know about being an LP:

1. *Providing Liquidity:* LPs deposit equal value of both tokens in a pair into the pool. For example, if you want to provide liquidity for an ETH/DAI pool, you'll need to deposit both ETH and DAI in a 50/50 ratio.
2. *Earning Fees:* LPs earn a share of the trading fees generated by the pool. These fees are distributed proportionally based on the amount of liquidity you've provided.
3. *Impermanent Loss:* One of the risks of being an LP is impermanent loss, which occurs when the price of the tokens in the pool changes significantly. This happens because the pool's algorithm rebalances the token ratio to maintain the constant product formula.

Example: If you provide liquidity to an ETH/DAI pool and the price of ETH doubles, the pool will rebalance to reflect the new price ratio. As a result, you might end up with more DAI and less ETH than you initially deposited, leading to impermanent loss.

Advantages of AMMs and Liquidity Pools

1. *No Order Books:* AMMs eliminate the need for order books, making trading more efficient and accessible.
2. *Continuous Liquidity:* Liquidity pools ensure that there's always liquidity available for trading, even for less popular tokens.
3. *Permissionless Access:* Anyone can become a liquidity provider and earn fees, regardless of their location or identity.
4. *Transparency:* All transactions and pool balances are recorded on the blockchain, making the system more transparent and trustworthy.

Real-World Example: Trading on Uniswap

Let's walk through a real-world example of how trading works on Uniswap, one of the most popular DEXs:

1. *Connect Your Wallet:* Connect your MetaMask wallet to Uniswap by clicking the "Connect Wallet" button.
2. *Select Tokens:* Choose the tokens you want to trade. For example, you might want to swap ETH for DAI.
3. *Enter Amount:* Enter the amount of ETH you want to swap. Uniswap will automatically calculate the amount of DAI you'll receive based on the current ratio in the liquidity pool.
4. *Review and Confirm:* Review the transaction details, including the estimated gas fee and slippage tolerance. Confirm the transaction in your wallet.
5. *Complete the Trade:* Once the transaction is confirmed, the ETH will be swapped for DAI, and the new tokens will appear in your wallet.

Liquidity pools and AMMs are revolutionizing the way we trade assets by making markets more accessible, efficient, and transparent. They empower individuals to participate in the financial system without relying on centralized intermediaries, creating a more inclusive and equitable economy.

Advantages of DEXs Over Centralized Exchanges

DEXs offer several key advantages over traditional centralized exchanges (CEXs):

1. *No Custody Risk:* On centralized exchanges, you must deposit your funds into the exchange's wallet, which makes them vulnerable to hacks or mismanagement. With DEXs, you retain control of your funds at all times.
2. *Privacy:* DEXs don't require KYC (Know Your Customer) verification, allowing you to trade anonymously.
3. *Global Access:* Anyone with an internet connection and a crypto wallet can use a DEX, regardless of their location.
4. *Lower Fees:* While gas fees on DEXs can be high during periods of network congestion, they often eliminate the high trading fees charged by centralized exchanges.
5. *Innovation:* DEXs are at the forefront of DeFi innovation, offering features like yield farming, liquidity mining, and governance tokens.

Example: If you're in a country where centralized exchanges are banned or restricted, you can still trade on a DEX like Uniswap or SushiSwap using just your crypto wallet.

Popular DEXs to Explore

Here are some of the most popular DEXs in the DeFi space:

1. *Uniswap:* The largest and most well-known DEX, Uniswap uses an AMM

model and supports a wide range of tokens. It's known for its simplicity and user-friendly interface.

2. *SushiSwap:* A fork of Uniswap, SushiSwap offers additional features like yield farming and staking rewards through its native token, SUSHI.
3. *PancakeSwap:* Built on Binance Smart Chain (BSC), PancakeSwap offers lower fees and faster transactions compared to Ethereum-based DEXs. It's particularly popular for trading BEP-20 tokens.
4. *Curve Finance:* Specializing in stablecoin trading, Curve Finance offers low slippage and high efficiency for stablecoin swaps.
5. *Balancer:* Balancer allows users to create custom liquidity pools with multiple tokens and varying weights, offering more flexibility for liquidity providers.

How to Start Trading on a DEX

Ready to start trading on a DEX? Here's a step-by-step guide:

1. *Set Up a Crypto Wallet:* If you haven't already, set up a crypto wallet like MetaMask and fund it with cryptocurrency.
2. *Choose a DEX:* Select a DEX that suits your needs. For beginners, Uniswap is a great starting point.
3. *Connect Your Wallet:* Connect your wallet to the DEX by clicking the "Connect Wallet" button and following the prompts.
4. *Select Tokens to Trade:* Choose the tokens you want to swap (e.g., ETH for DAI). Enter the amount you wish to trade.
5. *Review and Confirm:* Review the transaction details, including the estimated gas fee and slippage tolerance. Confirm the transaction in your wallet.
6. *Monitor Your Trade:* Once the transaction is confirmed, the tokens will be swapped, and the new tokens will appear in your wallet.
7. *Check Gas Fees:* Gas fees can vary depending on network congestion.

Use tools like Etherscan Gas Tracker to find the best time to trade.

8. *Set Slippage Tolerance:* Slippage is the difference between the expected price and the actual price of a trade. Set a reasonable slippage tolerance (e.g., 1–2%) to avoid failed transactions.
9. *Start Small:* Begin with a small trade to familiarize yourself with the process.

Understanding Risks

While DEXs offer many benefits, they also come with risks:

1. *Impermanent Loss:* Liquidity providers can experience impermanent loss if the price of the tokens in the pool changes significantly. This occurs when the value of your deposited tokens diverges from the value of holding them outside the pool.
2. *Smart Contract Risk:* DEXs rely on smart contracts, which can have vulnerabilities. If a smart contract is exploited, you could lose your funds.
3. *High Gas Fees:* On Ethereum-based DEXs, gas fees can be high during periods of network congestion. Consider using Layer 2 solutions or alternative blockchains like Binance Smart Chain to reduce fees.
4. *Scam Tokens:* DEXs allow anyone to list tokens, which means there's a risk of trading scam or low-quality tokens. Always research tokens before trading.

Example: If you provide liquidity to an ETH/DAI pool and the price of ETH doubles, you might experience impermanent loss because the pool's algorithm rebalances the token ratio.

The Future of Trading: A Decentralized World

DEXs are more than just a new way to trade—they're part of a broader movement to decentralize finance and empower individuals. By removing intermediaries, increasing transparency, and opening up access, DEXs are creating a more inclusive and equitable financial system. Whether you're a casual trader or a DeFi enthusiast, DEXs offer a world of opportunities to explore.

Imagine a future where anyone, anywhere, can trade assets seamlessly and securely, without needing permission from a central authority. That's the promise of DEXs—and it's already happening today.

In the next chapter, we'll explore yield farming and liquidity mining, diving into how you can earn rewards by providing liquidity to DeFi platforms. So, let's keep going—the decentralized future is waiting for you!

Chapter 7: Yield Farming and Liquidity Mining

If you've been exploring Decentralized Finance (DeFi), you've probably heard about yield farming and liquidity mining. These are two of the most popular ways to earn passive income in the DeFi world. But what exactly are they, and how do they work? In this chapter, we'll break down these concepts in simple terms, explain how you can get started, and discuss the risks and rewards involved. By the end, you'll have a clear understanding of how to earn rewards by participating in DeFi.

What Are Yield Farming and Liquidity Mining?

At their core, yield farming and liquidity mining are ways to earn rewards by providing *liquidity* (funds) to DeFi platforms. Think of it like this: when you deposit money into a bank, you earn interest. In DeFi, when you provide liquidity, you earn rewards—often in the form of cryptocurrency. But unlike traditional banking, DeFi rewards can be much higher, and you don't need permission from anyone to participate. Let's break it down further to make it easy to understand.

Yield Farming: Earning Rewards for Lending or Staking Crypto

Yield farming is a way to earn rewards by lending or staking your cryptocurrency in DeFi protocols. It's like putting your money to work in a decentralized version of a savings account, but with the potential for much higher returns. How it works:

1. *Lend Your Crypto:* You deposit your cryptocurrency into a DeFi platform (like Aave or Compound), and in return, you earn interest. The interest rates are often much higher than what you'd get from a traditional bank.
2. *Stake Your Crypto:* Some platforms allow you to "stake" your tokens, which means locking them up to support the network. In return, you earn rewards, usually in the form of more tokens.
3. *Earn Additional Tokens:* Many DeFi platforms offer extra rewards in the form of their native tokens. For example, if you lend your crypto on Compound, you might earn COMP tokens as a bonus.

Example: Let's say you deposit $1,000 worth of Ethereum (ETH) into Aave. You start earning interest on your deposit, and if Aave is running a yield farming program, you might also earn AAVE tokens as extra rewards.

Liquidity Mining: Earning Tokens for Providing Liquidity

Liquidity mining is a specific type of yield farming where you earn a platform's native tokens as rewards for providing liquidity. This is how many DeFi platforms incentivize users to contribute to their liquidity pools. How it works:

1. *Provide Liquidity:* You deposit pairs of tokens (e.g., ETH and DAI) into a liquidity pool on a platform like Uniswap or SushiSwap. These pools allow others to trade tokens, and in return, you earn rewards.

2. *Earn Trading Fees:* Every time someone trades using the pool, a small fee is charged, and you get a share of it.
3. *Earn Bonus Tokens:* Many platforms distribute their native tokens as extra rewards. For example, if you provide liquidity to Uniswap, you might earn UNI tokens.

Example: Imagine you deposit 1,000 worth of ETH and 1,000 worth of DAI into a liquidity pool on Uniswap. You'll earn a share of the trading fees generated by the pool, and if Uniswap is running a liquidity mining program, you might also earn UNI tokens as extra rewards.

How Do Yield Farming and Liquidity Mining Work?

Let's simplify how these processes work so you can easily understand and start earning rewards in DeFi. Think of yield farming and liquidity mining as ways to "rent out" your cryptocurrency to earn passive income. Here's a step-by-step breakdown of how it all comes together:

1. Provide Liquidity: Fueling the DeFi Ecosystem

When you provide liquidity, you're essentially depositing your cryptocurrency into a pool that others can use to trade. These pools are like shared wallets where people can swap one token for another (e.g., ETH for DAI). In return for providing liquidity, you earn rewards. How it works:

- *Deposit Token Pairs:* Most DeFi platforms require you to deposit pairs of tokens. For example, if you want to provide liquidity for an ETH/DAI pool, you'll need to deposit both ETH and DAI in equal value.
- *Liquidity Pools:* These pools are managed by smart contracts (automated programs) that ensure trades happen smoothly. The more liquidity in the pool, the easier it is for people to trade without causing big price swings.

By providing liquidity, you're helping the DeFi ecosystem function. Without liquidity, trading would be slow, expensive, and inefficient. In return for your contribution, you earn rewards.

2. Earn Rewards: Getting Paid for Your Contribution

Once you've provided liquidity, you start earning rewards. These rewards can come in several forms:

Trading Fees: Every time someone trades using the pool, a small fee is charged (usually around 0.3% on platforms like Uniswap). This fee is distributed to all liquidity providers based on their share of the pool.

Example: If the ETH/DAI pool generates $1,000 in trading fees in a week, and you contributed $110 in fees.

Interest: Some platforms, like Aave or Compound, pay interest on the tokens you deposit. This is similar to earning interest in a savings account, but the rates are often much higher.

Example: If you deposit $1,000 worth of USDC into Aave, you might earn 5% annual interest, paid in USDC.

Bonus Tokens: Many platforms reward liquidity providers with their native tokens. For example, if you provide liquidity to SushiSwap, you might earn SUSHI tokens as a bonus.

Example: If you deposit $1,000 into a SushiSwap liquidity pool, you might earn 10 SUSHI tokens per week as an extra reward.

3. Reinvest Your Earnings: Compounding Your Returns

One of the most powerful aspects of yield farming and liquidity mining is the ability to reinvest your earnings. This is called compounding, and it's a great way to grow your rewards over time. How Compounding works:

- Instead of withdrawing your rewards, you reinvest them into the same or another liquidity pool.
- Over time, your earnings grow exponentially because you're earning rewards on top of rewards.

Example: Let's say you earn $50 in trading fees and 10 SUSHI tokens in a week. Instead of cashing out, you invest the $50 and stake the SUSHI tokens to earn even more rewards. Over time, this can significantly increase your returns.

Why Are Yield Farming and Liquidity Mining Popular?

Yield farming and liquidity mining have taken the DeFi world by storm, and for good reason. These strategies offer a unique combination of high returns, accessibility, and community involvement that traditional finance simply can't match. Let's dive deeper into why these strategies are so popular and what makes them so appealing to both beginners and experienced crypto enthusiasts.

1. High Returns: Earn More Than Traditional Finance

One of the biggest draws of yield farming and liquidity mining is the potential for high returns. Unlike traditional savings accounts that offer interest rates as low as 0.01%, DeFi platforms can offer annual returns of 10%, 20%, or even higher. Here's why:

- *Competitive Interest Rates:* DeFi platforms often offer much higher interest rates than banks because they don't have the same overhead costs. Plus, they're competing for your funds, so they incentivize users with attractive rewards.
- *Multiple Income Streams:* When you provide liquidity, you can earn rewards from multiple sources, such as trading fees, interest, and bonus tokens. This creates a compounding effect that can significantly boost your earnings.

Example: Let's say you deposit $1,000 into a liquidity pool on Uniswap. You might earn 5% annual interest from trading fees and an additional 10% in UNI tokens as a bonus. That's a total return of 15%—far higher than what you'd get from a traditional savings account.

2. Empowerment: Take Control of Your Finances

Another reason yield farming and liquidity mining are so popular is the empowerment they offer. In traditional finance, you need to rely on banks, brokers, and financial advisors to manage your money. With DeFi, you're in full control.

- *No Middlemen:* DeFi eliminates the need for intermediaries. You don't need to open a bank account, pass a credit check, or pay high fees to a broker. All you need is a crypto wallet and some cryptocurrency.
- *Global Access:* DeFi is open to anyone with an internet connection, regardless of where they live. This is especially empowering for people in underbanked regions who don't have access to traditional financial services.

Example: Imagine a farmer in a remote village who can't access a bank. With DeFi, they can provide liquidity to a platform and earn rewards, giving them a way to grow their savings and improve their life.

3. Flexibility: Choose Your Own Adventure

Yield farming and liquidity mining offer a level of **flexibility** that traditional finance can't match. You can choose from a wide range of platforms, strategies, and tokens, depending on your risk tolerance and goals.

- *Diverse Platforms:* There are countless DeFi platforms to choose from, each offering different rewards and features. Whether you're looking for low-risk lending or high-reward yield farming, there's something for everyone.
- *Customizable Strategies:*You can mix and match different strategies to create a portfolio that suits your needs. For example, you might lend stablecoins for steady returns while also providing liquidity to a high-risk pool for higher rewards.

Example: Let's say you're a conservative investor. You might deposit stablecoins like DAI or USDC into a lending platform like Aave for steady interest. If you're more adventurous, you could provide liquidity to a volatile token pair on SushiSwap for higher potential returns.

4. Community Involvement: Be Part of Something Bigger

One of the most exciting aspects of yield farming and liquidity mining is the opportunity to get involved in the DeFi community. By participating, you're not just earning rewards—you're helping to build a new financial system.

- *Governance Tokens:* Many DeFi platforms distribute governance tokens as rewards. These tokens give you a say in how the platform is run, allowing you to vote on proposals and shape its future.
- *Supporting Innovation:* By providing liquidity, you're helping to fuel the

growth of the DeFi ecosystem. This creates a virtuous cycle where more users join, more liquidity is added, and more innovation happens.

Example: If you provide liquidity to Uniswap, you might earn UNI tokens as a reward. These tokens allow you to vote on important decisions, such as which new features to add or how to allocate funds.

Real-Life Example: Why People Love Yield Farming

Let's look at a real-life example to see why yield farming and liquidity mining are so popular:

1. *High Returns:* Sarah deposits $1,000 into a liquidity pool on SushiSwap. She earns 10% annual interest from trading fees and an additional 5% in SUSHI tokens. Her total return is 15%, far higher than her bank's 0.01% interest rate.
2. *Empowerment:* John lives in a country with limited access to banks. He uses DeFi to provide liquidity and earn rewards, giving him a way to grow his savings and improve his financial situation.
3. *Flexibility:* Maria is a cautious investor. She deposits stablecoins into Aave for steady returns but also allocates a small portion of her funds to a high-risk yield farming pool for higher potential rewards.
4. *Community Involvement:* Alex earns UNI tokens by providing liquidity to Uniswap. He uses these tokens to vote on platform proposals, giving him a sense of ownership and involvement in the DeFi ecosystem.

How to Get Started with Yield Farming

Ready to start earning rewards? Here's a simple step-by-step guide:

1. *Set Up a Crypto Wallet:* If you don't already have one, download a wallet like MetaMask and fund it with cryptocurrency.
2. *Choose a Platform:* Pick a DeFi platform that offers yield farming or liquidity mining. Popular options include Uniswap, SushiSwap, and Aave.
3. *Connect Your Wallet:* Connect your wallet to the platform by clicking the "Connect Wallet" button and following the instructions.
4. *Deposit Tokens:* Deposit pairs of tokens into a liquidity pool. For example, you might deposit ETH and DAI into an ETH/DAI pool.
5. *Start Earning:* Once your tokens are in the pool, you'll start earning rewards. Keep an eye on your earnings and consider reinvesting them to grow your returns.

Pro Tip: Start with a small amount of money to get comfortable with the process before committing larger sums.

What Are the Risks?

While yield farming and liquidity mining can be profitable, they also come with risks:

1. *Impermanent Loss:* This happens when the price of the tokens in your pool changes significantly. For example, if the price of ETH doubles, the pool will rebalance, and you might end up with less ETH than you started with.
2. *Smart Contract Risks:* DeFi platforms rely on smart contracts, which can have bugs or be hacked. If something goes wrong, you could lose your funds.

3. *Market Volatility:* The value of your tokens can go up or down quickly, especially if they're volatile assets like Ethereum or altcoins.
4. *High Fees:* On some platforms, especially those built on Ethereum, transaction fees (called gas fees) can be high, especially during busy times.

Example: If you provide liquidity to an ETH/DAI pool and the price of ETH drops by 50%, you might experience impermanent loss, meaning you'll have less ETH when you withdraw your funds.

The Big Picture: Why This Matters

Yield farming and liquidity mining are more than just ways to earn money—they're part of a bigger movement to make finance more open, transparent, and inclusive. By participating, you're helping to build a financial system that doesn't rely on banks or middlemen. Instead, it's powered by people like you, working together to create a fairer and more equitable economy.

Imagine a world where anyone, anywhere, can access financial services and earn rewards for contributing to the ecosystem. That's the promise of DeFi—and it's already happening today.

In the next chapter, we'll explore staking and governance in DeFi, where you can earn rewards by locking up your tokens and even have a say in how DeFi platforms are run. So, let's keep going—the decentralized future is waiting for you!

Chapter 8: Staking and Governance in DeFi

In the world of Decentralized Finance (DeFi), there's more to earning rewards than just yield farming and liquidity mining. Another powerful way to grow your crypto holdings is through staking and governance. These concepts might sound complex at first, but they're actually quite simple once you break them down. In this chapter, we'll explore what staking and governance are, how they work, and how you can get started. By the end, you'll understand how to earn rewards by locking up your tokens and even have a say in how DeFi platforms are run.

What Is Staking?

Staking is one of the most popular ways to earn passive income in the world of Decentralized Finance (DeFi). At its core, staking is a way to earn rewards by locking up your cryptocurrency to support a blockchain network. Think of it like putting your money in a high-yield savings account, but instead of earning interest from a bank, you're earning rewards directly from the blockchain itself. Let's break this down further to make it easy to understand.

How Does Staking Work?

Staking is a key feature of *Proof of Stake (PoS)* blockchains, which are designed to be more energy-efficient than traditional *Proof of Work (PoW)* blockchains like Bitcoin. Here's a step-by-step explanation of how staking works:

Lock Up Your Tokens: When you stake your tokens, you're essentially locking them up in a staking pool or validator node. These tokens are used to help secure the network and validate transactions. By staking, you're contributing to the network's security and efficiency.

- **Example:** Imagine you have 10 Ethereum (ETH) tokens. You decide to stake them on a platform like Lido. By doing this, you're helping to secure the Ethereum network and validate transactions.

Earn Rewards: In return for locking up your tokens, you earn rewards. These rewards are usually paid in the same cryptocurrency you staked, and the amount you earn depends on several factors, such as:

- The platform's reward rate (e.g., 5% annual return).
- The length of time you stake your tokens.
- The total amount of tokens staked in the network.

Example: If you stake 10 ETH on Lido and the platform offers a 5% annual return, you'll earn 0.5 ETH over the course of a year. After a year, you'll have 10.5 ETH.

Unlock Your Tokens: After a certain period (called the *staking period*), you can unlock your tokens and withdraw them, along with your rewards. Some platforms allow you to unstake your tokens at any time, while others require you to wait for a specific period.

- **Example:** If you stake your ETH for one year, you'll need to wait until the end of that year to withdraw your tokens and rewards. However, some platforms allow you to unstake earlier, but you might forfeit some of your rewards.

Why Stake Your Tokens?

Staking is popular for several reasons, making it an attractive option for both beginners and experienced crypto users:

- *Earn Passive Income:* Staking allows you to earn rewards without actively trading or managing your funds. It's a great way to grow your crypto holdings over time, especially if you're holding tokens for the long term.
- *Support the Network:* By staking your tokens, you're helping to secure and decentralize the blockchain network. This makes the network more robust, trustworthy, and resistant to attacks.
- *Low Risk:* Compared to other DeFi strategies like yield farming or liquidity mining, staking is generally considered lower risk because it doesn't involve complex strategies or volatile assets. However, it's not entirely risk-free (more on that later).
- *Energy Efficiency:* Staking is more environmentally friendly than traditional mining (used in PoW blockchains) because it doesn't require massive amounts of computational power.

Example: Staking Ethereum on Lido

Let's walk through a real-life example to make staking even clearer:

1. *Choose a Platform:* You decide to stake your Ethereum (ETH) on Lido, a

popular staking platform.

2. *Deposit Your Tokens:* You deposit 10 ETH into Lido's staking pool. These tokens are locked up and used to help secure the Ethereum network.
3. *Earn Rewards:* Lido offers a 5% annual return on staked ETH. Over the course of a year, you earn 0.5 ETH in rewards.
4. *Unlock Your Tokens:* After one year, you can unstake your ETH and withdraw your original 10 ETH plus the 0.5 ETH in rewards, giving you a total of 10.5 ETH.

What Is Governance?

In the world of Decentralized Finance (DeFi), governance is the process of making decisions about how a platform is run. Unlike traditional companies, where decisions are made by a small group of executives or a board of directors, DeFi platforms are often governed by their users. This is made possible through governance tokens, which give users the right to vote on proposals and shape the future of the platform. Let's dive deeper into what governance is, how it works, and why it's such an important part of the DeFi ecosystem.

How Does Governance Work?

Governance in DeFi is all about giving power to the people who use the platform. Here's a step-by-step breakdown of how it works:

Earn Governance Tokens: Many DeFi platforms distribute governance tokens to users as rewards for participating in the ecosystem. You can earn these tokens by:

- Providing liquidity to a platform (e.g., depositing tokens into a liquidity

pool).
- Staking your tokens.
- Participating in other activities, like yield farming or lending.

Example: If you provide liquidity to Uniswap, you might earn UNI tokens as a reward. These tokens give you the right to vote on proposals that affect the platform.

Vote on Proposals: Governance tokens allow you to vote on important decisions about the platform. These decisions can include:

- Adding new features or services.
- Changing the platform's rules or policies.
- Allocating funds (e.g., deciding how to spend the platform's treasury).
- Listing new tokens or assets on the platform.

Example: Let's say Uniswap proposes to add a new token (like DOGE) to its platform. As a UNI token holder, you can vote "yes" or "no" on this proposal.

Shape the Future: By participating in governance, you're helping to shape the future of the platform. Your votes can influence how the platform evolves, ensuring it meets the needs of its users and stays competitive in the fast-moving DeFi space.

- **Example:** If the Uniswap community votes to allocate funds to develop a new feature (like a mobile app), you've played a part in making that happen.

Why Is Governance Important?

Governance is a key feature of DeFi because it aligns the interests of the platform with the interests of its users. Here's why it matters:

1. *Decentralization:* Governance ensures that no single entity has control over the platform. Instead, decisions are made collectively by the community, making the platform more decentralized and resistant to censorship.
2. *Transparency:* All proposals and votes are recorded on the blockchain, making the governance process transparent and trustworthy. Anyone can see how decisions are made and who is influencing them.
3. *User Empowerment:* Governance gives users a voice in how the platform is run. This creates a sense of ownership and involvement, encouraging users to contribute to the platform's success.
4. *Innovation:* By allowing users to propose and vote on new ideas, governance fosters innovation. The best ideas rise to the top, ensuring the platform stays competitive and relevant.

Example: Governance on Uniswap

Let's walk through a real-life example to make governance even clearer:

1. *Earn UNI Tokens:* You provide liquidity to Uniswap and earn UNI tokens as a reward. These tokens give you the right to vote on proposals.
2. *Review a Proposal:* Uniswap proposes to add a new token (like DOGE) to its platform. The proposal outlines the benefits and risks of adding DOGE, as well as the potential impact on the platform.
3. *Cast Your Vote:* You review the proposal and decide whether to vote "yes" or "no." If you believe adding DOGE will benefit the platform, you vote "yes." If you're concerned about the risks, you vote "no."

4. *Shape the Future:* The proposal passes with a majority "yes" vote, and DOGE is added to Uniswap. You've played a part in shaping the future of the platform.'

What Are the Risks of Governance?

While governance is a powerful feature of DeFi, it's not without its challenges. Here are some risks to be aware of:

1. *Voter Apathy:* Not all users participate in governance, which can lead to decisions being made by a small group of active voters. This can result in decisions that don't reflect the broader community's interests.
2. *Concentration of Power:* If a small number of users hold a large portion of the governance tokens, they can dominate the decision-making process. This can undermine the decentralization of the platform.
3. *Complexity:* Governance can be complex, especially for beginners. Understanding proposals, evaluating their impact, and casting informed votes requires time and effort.
4. *Market Volatility:* The value of governance tokens can be volatile, which can impact your overall returns. If the price of the token drops significantly, the value of your voting power could also decrease.

How to Get Started with Staking and Governance

Ready to dive into the world of staking and governance in DeFi? These two activities are not only great ways to earn passive income but also allow you to play an active role in shaping the future of decentralized platforms. Whether you're a beginner or an experienced crypto user, this step-by-step guide will walk you through everything you need to know to get started.

Step 1: Choose a Platform

The first step is to choose a DeFi platform that offers staking and governance. Here are some popular options to consider:

1. *Lido:* A user-friendly platform for staking Ethereum (ETH) and earning rewards. Lido also offers governance opportunities through its LDO token.
2. *Aave:* A leading lending and borrowing platform that allows users to stake tokens and participate in governance using its AAVE token.
3. *Compound:* Another popular lending platform that offers staking and governance through its COMP token.
4. *Uniswap:* A decentralized exchange (DEX) that allows users to earn UNI tokens by providing liquidity and participate in governance.

How to Choose:

- *Reputation:* Stick to well-established platforms with a strong track record of security and reliability.
- *Rewards:* Compare the staking rewards and governance opportunities offered by different platforms.
- *Ease of Use:* Look for platforms with user-friendly interfaces, especially if you're a beginner.

Step 2: Deposit Your Tokens

Once you've chosen a platform, the next step is to deposit your tokens into a staking pool or validator node. Here's how to do it:

1. *Connect Your Wallet:* Most DeFi platforms require you to connect a crypto wallet like MetaMask. Follow the platform's instructions to connect

your wallet.

2. *Choose a Staking Pool:* Select the staking pool or validator node you want to deposit your tokens into. Make sure to read the platform's rules, including the staking period, reward rate, and any penalties for early withdrawal.
3. *Deposit Your Tokens:* Enter the amount of tokens you want to stake and confirm the transaction in your wallet. Your tokens will be locked up in the staking pool, and you'll start earning rewards.

Example: If you're using Lido, you might deposit 10 ETH into its staking pool. Lido will lock up your ETH and start paying you rewards in the form of stETH (staked ETH).

Step 3: Earn Rewards

Once your tokens are staked, you'll start earning rewards. Here's what you need to know:

1. *Reward Rate:* The reward rate varies depending on the platform and the tokens you're staking. For example, Lido might offer a 5% annual return on staked ETH.
2. *Compounding:* To maximize your returns, consider reinvesting your rewards. This is called compounding, and it allows you to earn rewards on top of rewards.
3. *Monitor Your Earnings:* Keep an eye on your staked tokens and rewards. Most platforms provide a dashboard where you can track your earnings and performance.

Example: If you stake 10 ETH on Lido and earn 0.5 ETH in rewards over a year, you can reinvest that 0.5 ETH to earn even more rewards in the future.

Step 4: Participate in Governance

If the platform offers governance tokens, you can use them to vote on proposals and shape the future of the platform. Here's how to get started:

1. *Earn Governance Tokens:* You can earn governance tokens by staking, providing liquidity, or participating in other activities on the platform. For example, if you provide liquidity to Uniswap, you might earn UNI tokens.
2. *Review Proposals:* Most platforms have a governance section where you can review active proposals. These proposals might include adding new features, changing platform rules, or allocating funds.
3. *Cast Your Vote:* Use your governance tokens to vote on proposals. Some platforms allow you to delegate your voting power to others if you don't want to vote directly.
4. *Shape the Future:* By participating in governance, you're helping to shape the future of the platform. Your votes can influence how the platform evolves and ensure it meets the needs of its users.

Example: If Uniswap proposes to add a new token (like DOGE) to its platform, you can use your UNI tokens to vote "yes" or "no" on the proposal.

Understanding Risks

While staking and governance offer many benefits, they also come with risks:

1. *Lock-Up Periods:* Some platforms require you to lock up your tokens for a certain period. During this time, you won't be able to access or trade your tokens.
2. *Slashing:* If the validator node you're staking with behaves maliciously, you could lose a portion of your staked tokens.
3. *Token Volatility:* The value of your tokens can go up or down, especially

if they're volatile assets like Ethereum or altcoins.

Example: If you stake 10 ETH and the price of ETH drops by 50%, the value of your staked tokens will also drop, even if you're earning rewards.

Tips for Success

To minimize risks and maximize your earnings, follow these tips:

1. *Choose Reputable Platforms:* Stick to well-established platforms with a strong track record of security and reliability.
2. *Diversify:* Spread your funds across multiple platforms and strategies to reduce risk.
3. *Monitor Your Investments:* Keep an eye on your staked tokens and the performance of the platform. Be ready to adjust your strategy if needed.
4. *Stay Informed:* Keep up with industry news and developments to stay informed about new opportunities and risks.

The Bigger Picture: Why This Matters

Staking and governance are more than just ways to earn money—they're part of a bigger movement to make finance more open and accessible. By participating, you're helping to build a financial system that doesn't rely on banks or middlemen. Instead, it's powered by people like you, working together to create a fairer and more transparent economy.

Imagine a world where anyone, anywhere, can access financial services and have a say in how they're run. That's the promise of DeFi—and it's already happening today.

In the next chapter, we'll explore the risks and challenges of DeFi, helping you understand how to navigate this exciting but complex space safely. So, let's keep going—the decentralized future is waiting for you!

Chapter 9: The Risks and Challenges of DeFi

Decentralized Finance (DeFi) is an exciting and innovative space, offering opportunities to earn high returns, take control of your finances, and participate in a global financial system. However, like any frontier, DeFi comes with its fair share of risks and challenges. In this chapter, we'll explore the potential pitfalls of DeFi, from smart contract vulnerabilities to market volatility, and provide practical tips to help you navigate this space safely. By the end, you'll have a clear understanding of the risks involved and how to protect yourself while exploring the world of DeFi.

1. Smart Contract Risks: The Foundation of DeFi

Smart contracts are self-executing programs that run on the blockchain. They power everything in DeFi, from lending platforms to decentralized exchanges. While they're incredibly powerful, they're not foolproof.

The Risks:

Bugs and Vulnerabilities:

- Smart contracts are written by humans, and humans make mistakes. If a smart contract has a bug or vulnerability, it can be exploited by hackers, leading to the loss of funds.

Code Immutability:

- Once a smart contract is deployed on the blockchain, it's nearly impossible to change. If a vulnerability is discovered, it can be difficult to fix without disrupting the platform.

Example: In 2021, the DeFi platform *Poly Network* was hacked, resulting in the theft of over $600 million worth of cryptocurrency. The hack was made possible by a vulnerability in the platform's smart contracts.

How to Protect Yourself:

- *Use Reputable Platforms:* Stick to well-established platforms with a strong track record of security.
- *Audit Reports:* Check if the platform's smart contracts have been audited by reputable firms.
- *Start Small:* Begin with a small amount of funds to test the platform before committing larger sums.

2. Market Volatility: The Rollercoaster of Crypto

Cryptocurrencies are known for their price swings. A token's value can skyrocket one day and plummet the next. This volatility can impact your investments in DeFi.

The Risks:

- *Impermanent Loss:* If you provide liquidity to a pool and the price of the tokens changes significantly, you could experience impermanent loss. This means you might end up with less of one token than you started with.
- *Collateral Liquidation:* If you borrow funds using crypto as collateral and the value of your collateral drops, your position could be liquidated, resulting in the loss of your collateral.

Example: Let's say you borrow $1,000 worth of DAI using 1 ETH as collateral. If the price of ETH drops by 50%, your collateral might no longer cover the loan, and your ETH could be liquidated.

How to Protect Yourself:

- *Use Stablecoins:* For lower risk, consider using stablecoins like DAI or USDC.
- *Monitor Your Positions:* Keep an eye on the value of your collateral and adjust your strategy if needed.
- *Diversify:* Spread your investments across multiple assets to reduce risk.

3. Regulatory Risks: The Uncertain Legal Landscape

The regulatory environment for DeFi is still evolving. Governments around the world are grappling with how to regulate this new financial system, and new rules could impact the availability or legality of certain platforms and services.

The Risks:

- *Bans and Restrictions:* Some countries have banned or restricted the use of DeFi platforms, making it difficult or illegal to participate.
- *Tax Implications:* The tax treatment of DeFi activities can be complex and varies by jurisdiction. Failure to comply with tax laws could result in penalties.

Example: In 2021, China banned all cryptocurrency transactions, making it illegal for citizens to use DeFi platforms.

How to Protect Yourself:

- *Stay Informed:* Keep up with regulatory developments in your country.
- *Consult a Professional:* If you're unsure about the tax implications of your DeFi activities, consult a tax professional.
- *Use VPNs (Cautiously):* If DeFi is restricted in your country, you might consider using a VPN, but be aware of the legal risks.

4. Scams and Fraud: The Dark Side of DeFi

The decentralized nature of DeFi makes it a target for scammers and fraudsters. From fake platforms to rug pulls, there are many ways to lose your funds if you're not careful.

The Risks:

- *Fake Platforms:* Scammers create fake DeFi platforms that look legitimate but are designed to steal your funds.
- *Rug Pulls:* Some projects attract investors with promises of high returns, only to disappear with the funds once they've raised enough money.

Example: In 2021, the DeFi project AnubisDAO raised $60 million from investors, only to disappear with the funds shortly after.

How to Protect Yourself:

- *Do Your Research:* Before investing in a platform or project, research its team, history, and community.
- *Avoid Unrealistic Promises:* If something sounds too good to be true, it probably is.
- *Use Trusted Sources:* Stick to platforms and projects recommended by trusted sources in the crypto community.

5. User Error: The Importance of Being Careful

DeFi platforms are complex, and even small mistakes can lead to big losses. From sending funds to the wrong address to misconfiguring a transaction, user error is a common risk in DeFi.

The Risks:

- *Lost Funds:* If you send funds to the wrong address or lose access to your wallet, your funds could be lost forever.
- *Failed Transactions:* If you misconfigure a transaction (e.g., set the wrong gas fee), it could fail, resulting in the loss of your funds.

Example: If you accidentally send ETH to a Bitcoin address, your funds will be lost because the two blockchains are incompatible.

How to Protect Yourself:

- *Double-Check Addresses:* Always double-check the address before sending funds.
- *Use Wallet Features:* Many wallets allow you to save frequently used addresses to avoid mistakes.
- *Start Small:* When trying a new platform or feature, start with a small amount of funds to minimize risk.

Tips for Navigating DeFi Safely

Decentralized Finance (DeFi) is an exciting and innovative space, but it's also a bit like the Wild West—full of opportunities, but also risks. To help you navigate this space safely and maximize your chances of success, here are some practical tips. Whether you're a beginner or an experienced user, these strategies will help you protect your funds and make informed decisions.

1. Educate Yourself: Knowledge Is Power

The first and most important step in navigating DeFi safely is to educate yourself. The more you know about how DeFi works, the better equipped you'll be to avoid pitfalls and seize opportunities. What you can do:

- *Learn the Basics:* Understand key concepts like liquidity pools, yield farming, staking, and governance.
- *Follow Reputable Sources:* Stay updated by following trusted crypto news outlets, blogs, and social media accounts.
- *Join Communities:* Participate in DeFi forums, Discord groups, and Telegram channels to learn from others and stay informed about new developments.

Example: If you're new to yield farming, take the time to understand how liquidity pools work and what impermanent loss is before diving in.

2. Use Reputable Platforms: Trust but Verify

Not all DeFi platforms are created equal. Some are well-established and secure, while others may be risky or even fraudulent. To minimize your risk, stick to reputable platforms with a strong track record. What you can do:

- *Research Platforms:* Before using a platform, research its team, history, and security measures. Look for platforms that have been audited by reputable firms.
- *Check Reviews:* Read reviews and feedback from other users to gauge the platform's reliability.
- *Start Small:* Even with reputable platforms, start with a small amount of funds to test the waters before committing larger sums.

Example: Platforms like Uniswap, Aave, and Compound are well-established and have a strong track record of security and reliability.

3. Diversify Your Investments: Don't Put All Your Eggs in One Basket

Diversification is a key strategy for managing risk in any investment, and DeFi is no exception. By spreading your funds across multiple platforms and strategies, you can reduce your exposure to any single point of failure. What you can do:

- *Spread Your Funds:* Instead of putting all your funds into one platform or strategy, spread them across multiple platforms, tokens, and activities.
- *Balance Risk and Reward:* Allocate a portion of your funds to lower-risk activities (like lending stablecoins) and a smaller portion to higher-risk activities (like yield farming).
- *Monitor Your Portfolio:* Regularly review your investments and adjust your strategy as needed.

Example: You might allocate 50% of your funds to lending stablecoins on Aave, 30% to staking on Lido, and 20% to yield farming on SushiSwap.

4. Stay Informed: Keep Your Finger on the Pulse

The DeFi space moves fast, with new platforms, trends, and risks emerging all the time. To stay ahead of the curve, it's important to stay informed. What you can do:

- *Follow News Outlets:* Keep up with the latest developments by following crypto news outlets like CoinDesk, Decrypt, and The Block.
- *Join Communities:* Participate in DeFi communities on platforms like Reddit, Discord, and Twitter to stay informed about new opportunities

and risks.

- *Set Up Alerts:* Use tools like Google Alerts or Twitter notifications to stay updated on specific topics or platforms.

Example: If you're using Uniswap, set up alerts for news about the platform to stay informed about updates, vulnerabilities, or new features.

5. Use Security Best Practices: Protect Your Funds

Security is paramount in DeFi. Because transactions are irreversible and there's no customer support to help you recover lost funds, it's crucial to take steps to protect your assets. What you can do:

- *Enable Two-Factor Authentication (2FA):* Use 2FA on all your accounts to add an extra layer of security.
- *Use Hardware Wallets:* Store your funds in a hardware wallet (like Ledger or Trezor) to protect them from hacks.
- *Keep Your Private Keys Secure:* Never share your private keys or seed phrases with anyone. Store them in a safe place, preferably offline.
- *Beware of Phishing Scams:* Be cautious of emails, messages, or websites that ask for your private keys or personal information. Always double-check URLs and only use official platforms.

Example: If you're using MetaMask, enable 2FA and store your seed phrase in a secure location, like a safe or a password manager.

6. Start Small: Test the Waters

If you're new to DeFi or trying out a new platform or strategy, it's a good idea to start small. This allows you to get comfortable with the process and understand the risks before committing larger sums. What you can do:

- *Use Small Amounts:* Start with a small amount of funds to test the platform or strategy.
- *Learn the Process:* Use this opportunity to learn how the platform works, how to navigate its interface, and how to manage your funds.
- *Gradually Increase:* Once you're comfortable and confident, you can gradually increase your investment.

Example: If you're trying yield farming for the first time, start with $100 instead of $1,000. This allows you to learn the ropes without risking too much.

7. Be Prepared for Volatility: Stay Calm and Patient

Cryptocurrencies are known for their volatility, and DeFi is no exception. Prices can swing dramatically in a short period, and it's important to stay calm and patient. What you can do:

- *Set Realistic Expectations:* Understand that DeFi investments can be highly volatile, and be prepared for ups and downs.
- *Avoid Panic Selling:* Don't make impulsive decisions based on short-term price movements. Stick to your strategy and focus on the long term.
- *Use Stablecoins:* For lower risk, consider using stablecoins like DAI or USDC, which are less volatile than other cryptocurrencies.

Example: If the price of ETH drops by 20% in a day, don't panic and sell. Instead, review your strategy and consider whether the fundamentals of your investment have changed.

The Bigger Picture: Why This Matters

Navigating DeFi safely is not just about protecting your funds—it's about building confidence and making informed decisions. By following these tips, you can minimize risks, maximize your chances of success, and fully enjoy the opportunities that DeFi has to offer.

Imagine a world where anyone, anywhere, can access financial services without relying on banks or middlemen. That's the promise of DeFi—and it's already happening today. But like any frontier, it requires caution, knowledge, and a willingness to learn.

In the next chapter, we'll explore the future of DeFi, looking at emerging trends and innovations that could shape the decentralized finance landscape in the years to come. So, let's keep going—the decentralized future is waiting for you!

Chapter 10: The Future of DeFi

Decentralized Finance (DeFi) has come a long way since its inception, evolving from a niche concept to a multi-billion-dollar ecosystem. But this is just the beginning. As technology advances and more people embrace decentralized finance, the future of DeFi looks brighter than ever. In this chapter, we'll explore the emerging trends and innovations that are shaping the future of DeFi. From Layer 2 solutions to cross-chain interoperability, we'll dive into what's next for this exciting space. By the end, you'll have a glimpse into the future of finance and how you can be part of it.

1. Layer 2 Solutions: Scaling DeFi for Mass Adoption

Layer 2 solutions are technologies built on top of existing blockchains (like Ethereum) to improve scalability and reduce transaction costs. They allow DeFi platforms to handle more users and transactions without congesting the main blockchain. Why it matters:

- *Lower Fees:* Layer 2 solutions significantly reduce gas fees, making DeFi more accessible to everyone.
- *Faster Transactions:* Transactions on Layer 2 networks are much faster, improving the user experience.
- *Mass Adoption:* By solving scalability issues, Layer 2 solutions pave the way for DeFi to reach a global audience.

Examples of Layer 2 Solutions:

- *Polygon (Matic):* A popular Layer 2 solution that offers fast and low-cost transactions for Ethereum-based DeFi platforms.
- *Optimism:* A scaling solution that uses optimistic rollups to increase Ethereum's throughput.
- *Arbitrum:* Another rollup-based solution that aims to make Ethereum more scalable and efficient.

Example: Imagine being able to trade on Uniswap or lend on Aave with transaction fees that cost just a few cents instead of tens or hundreds of dollars. That's the promise of Layer 2 solutions.

2. Cross-Chain Interoperability: Breaking Down Barriers

Cross-chain interoperability refers to the ability of different blockchains to communicate and interact with each other. This allows users to move assets and data seamlessly between blockchains. Why it matters:

- *Access to More Opportunities:* Cross-chain interoperability opens up a world of new opportunities by allowing users to access DeFi platforms on different blockchains.
- *Improved Liquidity:* By connecting different blockchains, cross-chain solutions can improve liquidity and reduce fragmentation in the DeFi ecosystem.
- *User Flexibility:* Users can choose the best blockchain for their needs without being locked into a single ecosystem.

Examples of Cross-Chain Solutions:

- *Polkadot:* A blockchain platform that enables interoperability between different blockchains.

- *Cosmos:* A network of interconnected blockchains that can communicate with each other.
- *Chainlink:* A decentralized oracle network that facilitates cross-chain communication.

Example: Imagine being able to use your Bitcoin on an Ethereum-based DeFi platform or move your assets from Binance Smart Chain to Solana without any hassle. That's the power of cross-chain interoperability.

3. Decentralized Identity (DID): Taking Control of Your Data

Decentralized Identity (DID) is a system that allows users to control their personal data and identity without relying on centralized authorities. In DeFi, DID can be used to verify identity, access services, and protect privacy. Why it matters:

- *Privacy:* DID gives users control over their personal data, reducing the risk of data breaches and identity theft.
- *Access to Services:* DID can be used to access DeFi services without needing to share sensitive information.
- *Trustless Systems:* DID enables trustless interactions, making DeFi more secure and transparent.

Examples of DID Projects:

- *Civic:* A decentralized identity platform that allows users to control their personal data.
- *SelfKey:* A blockchain-based identity system that enables users to manage their digital identity and access services.
- *Sovrin:* A decentralized identity network that provides secure and private identity solutions.

Example: Imagine being able to access a DeFi lending platform without needing to provide your Social Security number or other sensitive information. That's the promise of decentralized identity.

4. Institutional Adoption: Bringing DeFi to the Mainstream

Institutional adoption refers to the involvement of traditional financial institutions, such as banks, hedge funds, and corporations, in the DeFi space. This can bring more capital, credibility, and innovation to DeFi. Why it matters:

- *Increased Liquidity:* Institutional investors can bring significant capital to DeFi, increasing liquidity and stability.
- *Regulatory Clarity:* As institutions enter the space, regulators are more likely to provide clear guidelines, reducing uncertainty.
- *Mainstream Acceptance:* Institutional adoption can help DeFi gain mainstream acceptance and attract more users.

Examples of Institutional Involvement:

- *Grayscale:* A digital asset management firm that offers DeFi-focused investment products.
- *Goldman Sachs:* A major investment bank that has expressed interest in DeFi and blockchain technology.
- *MicroStrategy:* A publicly traded company that has invested heavily in Bitcoin and is exploring DeFi opportunities.

Example: Imagine a world where your local bank offers DeFi products, allowing you to earn interest on your savings without needing to use a crypto wallet. That's the potential of institutional adoption.

5. AI and Machine Learning: Smarter DeFi Platforms

Artificial Intelligence (AI) and Machine Learning (ML) are technologies that enable computers to learn from data and make decisions. In DeFi, AI and ML can be used to improve risk management, optimize trading strategies, and enhance user experiences. Why it matters:

- *Better Risk Management:* AI can analyze vast amounts of data to identify risks and opportunities, helping users make better decisions.
- *Automated Trading:* ML algorithms can optimize trading strategies, maximizing returns and minimizing risks.
- *Personalized Services:* AI can provide personalized recommendations and services, improving the user experience.

Examples of AI in DeFi:

- *Numerai:* A hedge fund that uses machine learning to make investment decisions.
- *Endor:* A predictive analytics platform that uses AI to provide insights for DeFi users.
- *Aavegotchi:* A DeFi project that uses AI to create unique and interactive NFT experiences.

Example: Imagine a DeFi platform that uses AI to analyze market trends and automatically adjust your portfolio to maximize returns. That's the future of AI in DeFi.

6. Regulatory Evolution: Building a Safer Ecosystem

As DeFi grows, regulators around the world are working to create frameworks that protect users while fostering innovation. This includes rules for anti-money laundering (AML), know-your-customer (KYC), and consumer protection. Why it matters:

- *User Protection:* Clear regulations can help protect users from fraud, scams, and other risks.
- *Increased Trust:* Regulatory clarity can increase trust in DeFi, attracting more users and investors.
- *Sustainable Growth:* A well-regulated DeFi ecosystem is more likely to achieve sustainable growth and mainstream adoption.

Examples of Regulatory Developments:

- *The EU's MiCA Regulation:* A proposed framework for regulating crypto assets and DeFi in the European Union.
- *The U.S. SEC's Guidance:* Ongoing efforts by the U.S. Securities and Exchange Commission to provide clarity on DeFi and crypto regulations.
- *Singapore's Regulatory Sandbox:* A program that allows DeFi projects to test their innovations in a controlled environment.

Example: Imagine a world where DeFi platforms are as safe and regulated as traditional banks, giving users peace of mind while still offering the benefits of decentralization. That's the goal of regulatory evolution.

The Bigger Picture: Why This Matters

The future of Decentralized Finance (DeFi) is not just about technological advancements or financial gains—it's about reshaping the way we think about money, trust, and access to financial services. The innovations we've explored—Layer 2 solutions, cross-chain interoperability, decentralized identity, institutional adoption, AI-driven platforms, and regulatory evolution—are all pieces of a larger puzzle. Together, they're building a financial system that is more open, inclusive, and equitable than anything we've seen before.

A World Without Barriers

Imagine a world where anyone, anywhere, can access financial services without needing permission from a bank or government. A world where:

- A farmer in a remote village can take out a loan to buy seeds and equipment, using their crypto as collateral.
- A small business owner in a developing country can accept payments from customers around the world, without paying exorbitant fees.
- A student can earn interest on their savings, even if they don't have a bank account.

This is the promise of DeFi—a world where financial services are borderless, permissionless, and accessible to all.

Empowering Individuals

At its core, DeFi is about empowerment. It's about giving individuals control over their money, their data, and their financial future. In the traditional financial system, power is concentrated in the hands of a few large institutions. In DeFi, power is distributed among the users.

- *Control Over Your Money:* With DeFi, you don't need to trust a bank to hold your funds. You can manage your money directly, using tools like crypto wallets and smart contracts.
- *Control Over Your Data:* Decentralized identity systems allow you to share only the information you choose, protecting your privacy and reducing the risk of data breaches.
- *Control Over Your Future:* By participating in DeFi, you're not just a user—you're a stakeholder. You can earn rewards, vote on proposals, and help shape the future of the platforms you use.

Building a Fairer System

The traditional financial system is riddled with inequalities. Millions of people around the world are unbanked or underbanked, meaning they don't have access to basic financial services like savings accounts, loans, or insurance. DeFi has the potential to change that.

- *Financial Inclusion:* DeFi opens up access to financial services for people who have been excluded from the traditional system. All you need is an internet connection and a crypto wallet.
- *Lower Costs:* By eliminating middlemen, DeFi reduces the cost of financial services, making them more affordable for everyone.
- *Transparency:* All transactions on the blockchain are public and verifiable, reducing the risk of fraud and corruption.

Example: Imagine a single mother in a developing country who can't access a bank loan because she doesn't have a credit history. With DeFi, she can use her crypto as collateral to take out a loan, giving her the funds she needs to start a small business and support her family.

The Role of Innovation

The innovations we've discussed—Layer 2 solutions, cross-chain interoperability, AI-driven platforms, and more—are not just technical achievements. They're tools for building a better financial system.

- *Layer 2 Solutions:* By reducing fees and increasing transaction speeds, Layer 2 solutions make DeFi more accessible to everyone, not just those who can afford high gas fees.
- *Cross-Chain Interoperability:* By connecting different blockchains, cross-

chain solutions create a more unified and efficient financial ecosystem.
- *AI and Machine Learning:* By analyzing data and optimizing strategies, AI can help users make better decisions and maximize their returns.
- *Regulatory Evolution:* By creating clear and fair regulations, governments can protect users while fostering innovation and growth.

The Promise of DeFi

The promise of DeFi is not just about making money—it's about creating a financial system that works for everyone. A system that is:

- *Open:* Anyone can participate, regardless of their location, income, or background.
- *Transparent:* All transactions are recorded on the blockchain, making the system more trustworthy and accountable.
- *Empowering:* Users have control over their money, their data, and their financial future.

Example: Imagine a world where a young entrepreneur in Africa can access the same financial tools and opportunities as a Wall Street investor. Where a retiree in Europe can earn interest on their savings without relying on a bank. Where a student in Asia can send money to their family overseas, instantly and cheaply. That's the world DeFi is building—and it's closer than ever.

Your Role in the Decentralized Future

The future of DeFi is bright, but it's not something that will happen on its own. It requires the participation of people like you—people who are willing to learn, experiment, and contribute to the ecosystem. Whether you're a beginner or an experienced user, there's a place for you in the decentralized future.

- *Start Small:* Begin with a small investment and learn the ropes. As you gain confidence, you can explore more advanced strategies.
- *Stay Informed:* Keep up with the latest developments in DeFi by following news outlets, joining communities, and participating in discussions.
- *Be Part of the Community:* Share your knowledge, ask questions, and contribute to the growth of the ecosystem. The more people who participate, the stronger DeFi will become.

In the next chapter, we'll wrap up our journey through DeFi with a conclusion and final thoughts. We'll reflect on what we've learned, discuss how you can take the next steps in your DeFi journey, and explore how you can contribute to the decentralized future. So, let's keep going—the decentralized future is waiting for you!

Conclusion and Final Thoughts

As we reach the end of this exploration into the world of Decentralized Finance (DeFi), it's time to reflect on what we've learned, the opportunities ahead, and the role you can play in shaping the future of finance. DeFi is more than just a technological innovation—it's a movement that promises to redefine how we think about money, trust, and access to financial services. This journey has taken us from the basics of blockchain and cryptocurrency to advanced strategies like yield farming, staking, and governance, as well as the risks, challenges, and innovations that are shaping the future of DeFi.

Now, let's tie it all together and look ahead to what's next.

The Revolution of DeFi

At its core, DeFi is revolutionary. It challenges the traditional financial system by removing intermediaries like banks and brokers and putting power directly into the hands of users. Through blockchain technology, smart contracts, and decentralized platforms, DeFi enables anyone with an internet connection to access financial services like lending, borrowing, trading, and earning interest—all without needing permission from a central authority. This shift has the potential to create a more open, transparent, and inclusive financial system, one that works for everyone, not just the privileged few.

We've seen how DeFi empowers individuals by giving them control over their money and data. It opens up opportunities for people who have been excluded from traditional finance, such as the unbanked and underbanked populations. It reduces costs, increases transparency, and fosters innovation. But perhaps most importantly, DeFi is a community-driven movement. It's built by people like you—people who are willing to learn, experiment, and contribute to the ecosystem.

The Opportunities and Challenges

Throughout this book, we've explored the many opportunities DeFi offers. From earning passive income through yield farming and staking to participating in governance and shaping the future of platforms, DeFi provides a wide range of ways to grow your wealth and take control of your financial future. However, these opportunities come with risks. Smart contract vulnerabilities, market volatility, impermanent loss, and regulatory uncertainty are just a few of the challenges you need to navigate.

The key to success in DeFi is education and caution. By understanding how DeFi works, staying informed about new developments, and following best practices, you can minimize risks and maximize your chances of success. Start small, diversify your investments, and always prioritize security. Remember, DeFi is still a young and evolving space, and it's important to approach it with both curiosity and care.

The Future of DeFi

The future of DeFi is incredibly exciting. Innovations like Layer 2 solutions, cross-chain interoperability, decentralized identity, and AI-driven platforms are paving the way for a more efficient, inclusive, and equitable financial system. Layer 2 solutions are making DeFi more accessible by reducing fees and increasing transaction speeds. Cross-chain interoperability is breaking down barriers between blockchains, creating a more unified ecosystem. Decentralized identity is giving users control over their data, while AI is optimizing strategies and improving user experiences.

At the same time, institutional adoption and regulatory evolution are bringing DeFi closer to mainstream acceptance. As traditional financial institutions and governments engage with DeFi, we can expect clearer regulations, increased liquidity, and greater trust in the ecosystem. These developments are not just about making DeFi more efficient—they're about building a financial system that works for everyone.

Your Role in the Decentralized Future

The decentralized future is not something that will happen on its own—it requires the participation of people like you. Whether you're a beginner taking your first steps into DeFi or an experienced user exploring advanced strategies, you have a role to play in shaping this future. Here's how you can get involved:

1. *Start Small and Learn:* If you're new to DeFi, start with small investments

and take the time to learn how everything works. Experiment with different platforms and strategies, and don't be afraid to ask questions.

2. *Stay Informed:* The DeFi space moves fast, with new platforms, trends, and risks emerging all the time. Stay informed by following reputable news outlets, joining communities, and participating in discussions.
3. *Be Part of the Community:* DeFi is a community-driven movement, and your participation matters. Share your knowledge, ask questions, and contribute to the growth of the ecosystem. The more people who participate, the stronger DeFi will become.
4. *Advocate for Change:* As DeFi grows, it's important to advocate for fair and clear regulations that protect users while fostering innovation. By engaging with policymakers and regulators, you can help shape the future of DeFi in a positive way.

The Promise of DeFi

The promise of DeFi is not just about making money—it's about creating a financial system that works for everyone. A system that is:

- *Open:* Anyone can participate, regardless of their location, income, or background.
- *Transparent:* All transactions are recorded on the blockchain, making the system more trustworthy and accountable.
- *Empowering:* Users have control over their money, their data, and their financial future.

Imagine a world where a young entrepreneur in Africa can access the same financial tools and opportunities as a Wall Street investor. Where a retiree in Europe can earn interest on their savings without relying on a bank. Where a student in Asia can send money to their family overseas, instantly and cheaply. That's the world DeFi is building—and it's closer than ever.

Final Thoughts

The decentralized future is not just a dream—it's a reality that's being built right now, by people like you. Whether you're a beginner taking your first steps into DeFi or an experienced user exploring advanced strategies, you're part of a movement that's reshaping the world of finance.

So, what are you waiting for? The decentralized future is waiting for you. Take the next step, explore the possibilities, and be part of the revolution. Together, we can build a financial system that is more open, inclusive, and equitable than anything we've seen before.

Thank you for joining me on this journey. Now, let's go out there and make the decentralized future a reality!

Bonus Content: Tools, Resources, and Next Steps for Your DeFi Journey

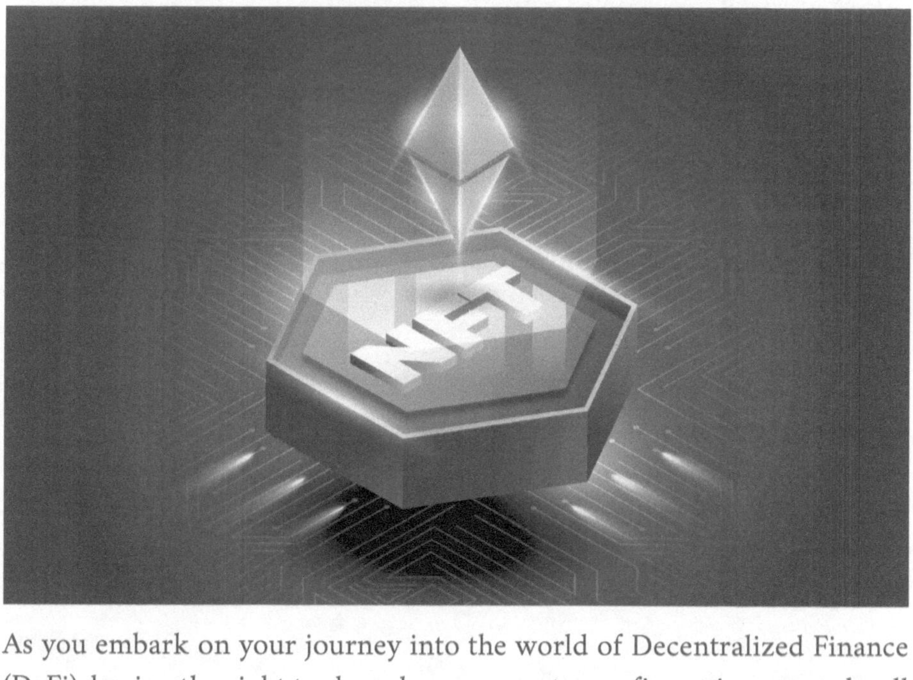

As you embark on your journey into the world of Decentralized Finance (DeFi), having the right tools and resources at your fingertips can make all the difference. This bonus content is designed to provide you with practical guidance, helpful tools, and actionable next steps to help you navigate the DeFi space with confidence. Whether you're a beginner or an experienced user, these resources will help you stay informed, make smarter decisions, and maximize your success in DeFi.

1. Essential Tools for DeFi

To get started in DeFi, you'll need a few essential tools. Here's a list of the most important ones:

Crypto Wallets: A crypto wallet is your gateway to DeFi. It allows you to store, send, and receive cryptocurrencies, as well as interact with DeFi platforms.

- **MetaMask:** A popular browser extension and mobile wallet for Ethereum-based DeFi platforms.
- **Trust Wallet:** A mobile wallet that supports multiple blockchains and tokens.
- **Ledger/Trezor:** Hardware wallets for added security.

DeFi Platforms: These are the platforms where you can lend, borrow, trade, and earn rewards.

- **Uniswap:** A decentralized exchange (DEX) for swapping tokens.
- **Aave:** A lending and borrowing platform.
- **Compound:** Another lending platform that offers governance opportunities.
- **SushiSwap:** A DEX with additional features like yield farming and staking.

Analytics Tools: These tools help you track your investments, monitor market trends, and make informed decisions.

- **DeFi Pulse:** Tracks the total value locked (TVL) in DeFi platforms.
- **Zapper:** A dashboard for managing your DeFi portfolio.
- **Etherscan:** A blockchain explorer for tracking transactions on

Ethereum.

Gas Fee Trackers: Gas fees can be a major expense on Ethereum-based platforms. These tools help you find the best time to transact.

- **GasNow:** Provides real-time gas price estimates.
- **Etherscan Gas Tracker:** Tracks gas prices and network congestion.

2. Educational Resources

The DeFi space is constantly evolving, and staying informed is key to success. Here are some resources to help you keep up with the latest developments:

Websites and Blogs:

- **CoinDesk:** A leading source of crypto and DeFi news.
- **Decrypt:** Covers the latest trends and developments in DeFi.
- **The Defiant:** A newsletter and website focused on DeFi.

YouTube Channels:

- **Coin Bureau:** Provides in-depth reviews and tutorials on DeFi platforms.
- **Ivan on Tech:** Covers a wide range of crypto and DeFi topics.
- **Finematics:** Explains complex DeFi concepts in simple terms.

Podcasts:

- **Bankless:** A podcast and newsletter focused on DeFi and the broader crypto ecosystem.
- **The Defiant Podcast:** Features interviews with DeFi leaders and innovators.
- **Unchained:** Covers the latest news and trends in crypto and DeFi.

Communities:

- **Reddit:** Subreddits like r/DeFi and r/CryptoCurrency are great for discussions and advice.
- **Discord:** Many DeFi projects have active Discord communities where you can ask questions and connect with other users.
- **Twitter:** Follow DeFi leaders, developers, and influencers for real-time updates and insights.

3. Next Steps for Your DeFi Journey

Now that you have the tools and resources, here are some actionable next steps to help you get started and grow in the DeFi space:

1. *Set Up Your Wallet:* If you haven't already, set up a crypto wallet like MetaMask or Trust Wallet. Fund it with a small amount of cryptocurrency to get started.
2. *Explore DeFi Platforms:* Start exploring different DeFi platforms, such as Uniswap, Aave, and Compound. Try out different strategies, like lending, staking, and yield farming, to see what works best for you.
3. *Diversify Your Investments:* Spread your funds across multiple platforms and strategies to reduce risk. Consider allocating a portion of your funds to lower-risk activities (like lending stablecoins) and a smaller portion

to higher-risk activities (like yield farming).

4. *Stay Safe:* Follow security best practices, such as enabling two-factor authentication (2FA), using hardware wallets, and keeping your private keys secure. Always double-check addresses and be cautious of phishing scams.
5. *Keep Learning:* The world of DeFi is constantly evolving, and there's always more to learn. Take the time to explore new platforms, strategies, and innovations, and don't be afraid to experiment.
6. *Join the Community:* Participate in DeFi communities on platforms like Reddit, Discord, and Twitter. Share your knowledge, ask questions, and contribute to the growth of the ecosystem.

4. Glossary of Key Terms

To help you navigate the DeFi space, here's a glossary of key terms you'll encounter:

- **AMM (Automated Market Maker):** A type of decentralized exchange that uses algorithms to set prices and facilitate trades.
- **APY (Annual Percentage Yield):** The annual rate of return on an investment, including compound interest.
- **Collateral:** Assets used to secure a loan or other financial obligation.
- **Gas Fees:** Transaction fees on the Ethereum network.
- **Governance Tokens:** Tokens that give holders the right to vote on proposals and shape the future of a platform.
- **Impermanent Loss:** A temporary loss of funds that can occur when providing liquidity to a pool.
- **Liquidity Pool:** A pool of tokens locked in a smart contract to facilitate trading on a DEX.
- **Staking:** Locking up cryptocurrency to support a blockchain network and earn rewards.

- **Yield Farming:** Earning rewards by providing liquidity to DeFi platforms.

The world of DeFi is full of opportunities, but it's also complex and ever-changing. As you take your first steps into this exciting space, remember to approach it with curiosity, caution, and a willingness to learn. Start small, stay informed, and don't be afraid to ask questions. The DeFi community is full of passionate and knowledgeable people who are eager to help newcomers.

Most importantly, remember that you're part of a movement that's reshaping the world of finance. By participating in DeFi, you're helping to build a more open, inclusive, and equitable financial system—one that works for everyone, not just the privileged few.

www.ingramcontent.com/pod-product-compliance
Lightning Source LLC
LaVergne TN
LVHW090419210926
848480LV00002B/616
* 9 7 9 8 2 3 0 7 4 7 1 5 4 *